REVEALED

To: Patricia Reyes

SAMUEL G. JONES

REVEALED

Discovering God's Will for Our Lives

TATE PUBLISHING & *Enterprises*

Published by Tate Publishing & Enterprises, LLC
127 E. Trade Center Terrace | Mustang, Oklahoma 73064 USA
1.888.361.9473 | www.tatepublishing.com

Tate Publishing is committed to excellence in the publishing industry. The company reflects the philosophy established by the founders, based on Psalm 68:11,
"The Lord gave the word and great was the company of those who published it."

Cover design by April Marciszewski
Interior design by Christina Hicks

Published in the United States of America

ISBN: 978-1-61777-527-7
1. Religion / Christian Life / Inspirational
2. Religion / Biblical Biography / General
11.04.11

Table of Contents

Preface

In my time as a Christian and minister, I have heard it said on countless occasions, "Lord! What is your will for my life? What do you want me to do? What career or profession should I choose? What is my purpose?" Many who call on the name of God have heard a common refrain. Cries have gone forth from the lips of those who love God as they search for meaning and purpose in their lives. They want to know that they are on the right track and heading in the right direction.

Many a saint has uttered these words in desperation and frustration only to walk away still empty and void of an answer. They ask friends, spiritual leaders, mentors, and family members only to be bombarded with a myriad of opinions but are often left in the same position. It is my opinion that God has not left us to wander through life in a quandary with no joy or assurance of his will for our lives. I believe that we can know with much more certainty than we presently have of the will of God for our lives.

No man can know the mind of God, but examples from the Scriptures show us that the will of God was revealed in obvious ways in the lives of his people that we read of in the Bible. We can, of course, see his will more clearly for them as we look back with 20/20 vision at the lives of biblical characters. But if we learn to look more closely and with discernment, I believe there are telltale signs that God gives us to know the direction he has for our lives. I do not pretend to claim that any man can know the definitive will of God, but that God does reveal some things to us of his out-workings. If we learn to pay attention, we can find comfort, joy, and peace knowing that we are walking in the will of God for our lives.

It is my prayer that this book serves to bring comfort, joy, and peace to all who call on his name knowing that he has a purpose and will for each of us. We can then move forward with greater confidence and assurance as we walk in his will and in keeping with the movement of his hand in our daily lives. God has not spun the world for one last time and then stepped back, waiting for it all to end. He is still alive and working. This knowledge can cause us to say, "Speak, Lord; for thy servant heareth" (1 Samuel 3:9, KJV).

This book is written in two sections to assist the reader in learning to see the revealed will of God for their own life. The first section is an examination of the lives of eight Old Testament characters to see how God was moving them toward his revealed will. We will examine the lives of Joseph, Moses, Jephthah, Ruth, Samuel, David, Abigail, and Amos. In each life, there are a number of indicators to alert the individual that God is moving them in a certain direction. There are five indicators, but not all may appear in the life of every person. Let the reader learn to look at these in his/her own life and peer closely to see how God may be moving them toward his revealed will for their lives. Providence, passion (drive), natural abilities, personality traits, and urging (calling) are indicators that reveal the direction the Lord may have for each person's life.

The second section is a practical guide to help the reader look at his/her own life to make sense of the often overlooked movements of God, the obstacles that hinder our understanding of the will of God for our lives, and encouragement to press on and trust him to keep his promise to use each saint for his glory. Be assured that God has a plan for your life and will fulfill it in his time.

SECTION ONE: LIFE EXAMINATIONS

Joseph

Joseph's life is a model to show us that God is still on the throne and directing the affairs of men.

Providence

Providence is defined as divine care or guidance. We can know that God is working or allowing events to take place in our lives to move us to that place where we are walking in his revealed will. Simply put, providence is when things happen to you and are not manufactured of your own accord. When we act, there are consequences that may be positive or negative. To have confidence that you are being moved toward his will is to understand what is going on when things happen in your life that you did not have anything to do with.

Joseph had nothing to do with the household he was born into or being born of the favored wife, Rachel. He was born into the lineage of Abraham, to whom the promise had been given. God declared to the patriarch: "And I will make thee exceeding fruitful, and I will make nations of thee, and kings shall come out of thee" (Genesis 17:6, KJV).

God placed him in the right family (Abraham was the one to whom the promise was made) with the right father (Jacob, the one chosen by God) and mother (Rachel, the one favored by Jacob). He was placed on a path that led him into Egypt, thus putting him in position to fulfill the declaration that God made to Abraham when he called him from his father's home: "And he said unto Abram, Know of a surety that thy seed shall be a stranger in a land that is not theirs, and shall serve them; and they shall afflict them four hundred years" (Genesis 15:13, KJV).

When things happen beyond our control, we can know that we are being moved by God's hand. Providence can manifest in several ways, such as trials, circumstances, or the actions of other people as it affects your life. His being born of the favored wife is an example of providence being manifested in circumstances. His father's partiality is an example of people's actions in your life that are beyond your control. Providence, in such fashion, can be seen by the keen eye and spirit as one observes how people that come into their lives begin to exert influence and actions that the recipient has nothing to do with. His father's actions led to such a rift in the family that his brothers were moved to wanting to kill him but settled on selling him to the Ishmaelites who just happened to be on their way to Egypt. None of this was of his doing; it just happened to him.

The believer needs to be careful at this point and understand that providence does not always mean that things will be pleasant and easy. Sometimes the very people or circumstances that God may bring into your life or allow in your life may bring you a great deal of pain and discomfort. But nonetheless, God is still working to bring about his will in the life of the believer.

This reality is expressed poignantly in Hannah Hurnard's, Hinds' Feet on High Places. In this story the chief character, Much Afraid, is given companions to travel with her on her journey to the High Places. The companions chosen by the Chief Shepherd are certainly not the ones she would have chosen, but the Shepherd knows that they are the ones that she needs in order to complete her journey:

> "Here are the two guides whom I promised," said the Shepherd quietly. "From now on until you are over the steep and difficult places, they will be your companions and helpers." … "They are good teachers; indeed, I have few better. As for their names …" said he, motioning toward the first of the silent figures, "is named Sorrow." And the other is her twin sister, Suffering.
>
> pp. 65-66

As we move along the path to the place of God's will, companions such as these will be assigned to help and guide us. They are not the ones we would desire, but they are the ones that the Shepherd knows that we need. Such companions accompanied Joseph.

Once he was in Egypt, a man named Potiphar bought him. It is interesting that any man could have bought Joseph, but God allowed him to be bought by the right person who was in the right position and place to give him access to where God would eventually want him for this season of his life: in jail. Potiphar saw God's favor upon Joseph and gave him the position as overseer over his house. One day, as he was about his master's business, an unexpected event occurred. Potiphar's wife attempted to seduce him and get him to sleep with her, and in his refusal to sin against God and his master, he found himself in jail, as she lied and told her husband that Joseph had attempted to rape her. Jail may seem like a really bad place for him to be, but it was a part of God's will, for while in jail, he made connections with people whom he may have otherwise never met.

Providence may be an indicator of how God is moving in our lives to place us in the position of his divine will, but our individual God-given personality traits may serve as indicators as well. When we have been endowed with traits that stand out or are noticed by others, these may be signs that God is moving us by use of our personality to that place of his divine will.

Personality Traits

Potiphar noticed some things in Joseph that propelled the young man to a place of prominence. Genesis records that Potiphar noticed that God was with him and that he was prosperous. How could Potiphar know these things? Keep in mind that Joseph was a young boy; poor, with only the clothes on his back; and a slave. So how did Potiphar surmise that God was with him and that he was prosperous? Let me attempt to explain from my observation and study. The fact that Joseph's devotion to God was evident can only be seen in his personality, character, and actions. Joseph worked and lived in the presence of Potiphar, and there was rarely an occasion when he found himself away from his master. It would be difficult in such a situation for a person to hide their true self from others while living in such a fish bowl. Joseph evidently proved that he was a person of good character, even-tempered, trustworthy, and gentle. He demonstrated that he was a worshiper of God and made his devotion known by deeds, such as consistency in prayer and in his conversation. As Potiphar witnessed Joseph on a daily basis, I am sure that he took note that he had never encountered anyone like Joseph before.

His prosperity had nothing to do with his own personal possessions, for he had none, but it had everything to do with God's blessings and favor upon him in whatever endeavor he put his hands to do. His personality was one of a person who could be a blessing to others and influence them in proper ways. Seeing this, Potiphar was moved to promote Joseph so that whatever Joseph possessed could rub off on the possessions that were under his charge and cause them to increase. God can use your personality to be so positive and an apparent blessing that others will be moved to want to be in your presence and revel in the sunlight of God's blessing as they reflect off of you.

In spite of God's favor, Joseph still found himself in jail for something that he did not do. While in jail it was evident to all that met Joseph that he was a special man. His godliness, good character, and magnetic personality shined through to the point that he was entrusted with the operation of the prison and was placed over the care of all the prisoners. What can possibly explain this? I suggest that it was his personality traits. Keep in mind and understand that he started off in jail just like everyone else, but there was something about him that caught the eye of the keeper of the prison and caused him to extend favor and responsibilities to Joseph.

No mention is made of Joseph purposely seeking to change and improve his personality, as some may have to do; he was simply being himself. Your personality may be a tool God uses to move you to the place where he wants you to be. Some may have negative and unpleasant personalities that truly may need changing. But when your natural personality opens doors for you and places you in positions that there really is no way to explain how you got there, God may be moving you into position.

Natural Abilities

Joseph could probably recall the first time he became aware of his God-given natural ability to interpret dreams. Up until that point, it had only gotten him nothing but grief and strained relationships. Whatever your ability and no matter how unrewarding it may appear to be, it is important to know that if God has gifted you in some area, he has done so for a purpose, which will be revealed in his time. We must patiently wait for the day that the purpose is revealed and use our ability to God's glory as often as possible until that time. There may have been many times when he wished he did not have this ability or sought to suppress it and keep quiet about it. Every individual must learn to examine themselves in search of their God-given ability that is natural for them but can be used to aid others. Find that area, and use it as often as possible, and God will use it to lead you to the place of his revealed will for your life.

The time came when Joseph found himself in jail, and the ability that he learned to dread and suppress came to the forefront in his life. During his time in jail, he met two men that were servants of the king: a baker and a butler. They were in prison along with Joseph because each had displeased the king in some fashion. A night came when both men dreamed dreams that they could not interpret, and, wouldn't you know it, there was Joseph, who had been gifted by God to interpret dreams.

Our natural abilities or area of giftedness is an indicator that we must not ignore in discovering God's revealed will for our lives. Joseph was naturally gifted by God to interpret dreams. He had been doing it since he was a kid, which, of course, his family did not appreciate.

He interpreted each man's dream and asked only that he be remembered by the butler, who would be restored to his former position as cupbearer to the king. The baker was beheaded as Joseph told him, according to the interpretation of his dream. The butler was restored and forgot all about Joseph.

Trials and Adversity

Life can be full of trials and adversities and can break your spirit if you see no purpose for them or end to them. Joseph endured many trials over the course of his young life. He languished in jail, and had it not been for his visions of God's will for his life, he could have well given up, lay down upon his bed, and waited for death. He could have become bitter and turned his heart from the God of his fathers, but he held on because he knew God had something better for him. He had shown him his will years earlier when he was yet in his father's home. Donna Partow, in her book Becoming a Vessel God Can Use, speaks of the need to maintain faith in the face of adversity:

> The Bible says we are to consider such trials to be pure joy, knowing that they are conforming us into the image of Christ. Indeed, the only way we can survive with our sanity and our faith intact is to refuse to demand an explanation from God. The moment we start functioning in the realm of "Why," we're in the danger zone. The only safe and sane questions to ask are: "What now, Lord?" "Where do you want me to go from here?"
>
> p. 130

Joseph appears to have had this kind of spirit and mindset. He knew God was a promise keeper and faithful, so he kept going and kept hope alive in his heart.

In Genesis 37:5–11, Joseph had two dreams that one day his father, mother, and brethren would bow before him. These dreams were not born of his own selfish pride, but they were the revealed will of God that one day Joseph would stand superior and in a position of honor before his family. He had no way of knowing how or when this would happen, but he believed God would be true to his word. The time of these dreams to their fulfillment would span about thirteen years. He was seventeen when the dreams came to him and thirty when he was finally lifted out of the pit of jail and promoted to the highest office in the land next to Pharaoh.

His trials were represented by being hated and despised by his brethren, plotted against for murder, sold to a traveling band, sold into slavery, falsely accused and lied about, thrown into jail, forgotten and betrayed by one whom he had helped, and left to languish for an additional two years. But when God has a plan for your life, his plan will come to pass if we wait on him. A day came when Joseph was still in jail and Pharaoh was troubled by a series of dreams that no one could interpret. The butler, who had forgotten Joseph, suddenly remembered him as being one who had been gifted by God to interpret dreams. Joseph was called to interpret the dreams of Pharaoh and was rewarded and promoted to prime minister of the land. Pharaoh declared that Joseph should be ruler of his house and over all the people and sent runners before Joseph's chariot to declare to the people to bow their knee.

Who but a trusting child of God could have seen this coming? That is what Joseph was: faithful. He did not know the details, but he knew that God, through the dreams, had made a promise. Let Joseph be a lesson for us that God has a will for us and will fulfill his will, but it is up to the individual believer to see his will, trust that he is moving, and be faithful in the meantime.

Moses

Moses was called to be a savior and deliverer of his people, Israel, but who of his contemporaries could have seen this coming or even he himself as he walked in his own shoes? His life gives clues to help those who walk this earth today to know that God has not left us without glimpses into his will for our lives.

Providence

The providence of God is evident in the life of Moses by his birth to a Hebrew mother, divine protection from slaughter at the hands of Pharaoh, and his return to his mother to be nurtured and raised. Consider the many seeming coincidences that took place in the birth and preservation of Moses. He was born at a crucial juncture in the history of his people. They were slaves, grossly mistreated, and Pharaoh had ordered the death of all infant males.

God had spoken through Joseph in Genesis 50:24 and reiterated the promise to Abraham to return his people to the land of Palestine so they may possess it. But the Israelites, who started out as guests in Egypt, became slaves and were harshly treated by the new pharaoh, who knew not Joseph (Exodus 1:8–14). God kept his promise to Abraham by raising up a deliverer for his people in the person of Moses. Jochebed, Moses's mother, was with child during adverse and difficult times. Pharaoh had ordered the death of all Hebrew baby boys, and she was in a dilemma with what to do to protect her infant son. The scene of Hebrew mothers in Egypt seeking any means to protect their infant sons must have been chilling. Some may have tried to escape Egypt; others may have plead with the executioners for the lives of their children, while others fought to the death, but what did Jochebed do? Exodus 2:2 records the desperate actions of the young mother—how she made an ark of bulrushes daubed with slim and pitch, put the child in it, and set it in the Nile River. We can only imagine the anxiety Jochebed felt knowing that to keep him at home meant certain death but to set him in the river wrought with perils was equally as dangerous. Wow! What faith—to trust God for his providential care in the face of unenviable choices.

God's providence is sometimes most evident in the midst of trials and adversities. It is in those times that it becomes crystal clear to believers that the only way out of their situation is through the divine intervention of Almighty God. With this knowledge of the hand of God being with her, Jochebed acts in a fashion that may be viewed by some as an act of desperation. Some may look at her actions as that of a desperate mother, but providence causes it to be viewed differently. The sparing of Moses's life had nothing to do with him but everything to do with God's protection and intervention.

The Nile poses many dangers. There were dangers of crocodiles, snakes, and other wildlife. There was a danger of any Egyptian fishing along its banks of discovering the child, and there was danger of the basket not being properly sealed and sinking into the river. But Moses could look back at his birth and preservation alone and know that God had a purpose for his life. How else can one explain Pharaoh's daughter finding Moses's basket and keeping him in light of her father's edict? When things happen to you without your interference, it can best be described as providence. John J. Davis writes in Moses and the Gods of Egypt:

> What looked like a potentially disastrous situation turned out, under the providence of God, to be the means by which God could prepare Moses for the great challenge which was ahead? The tragic events brought about by Pharaoh and the resulting good which was accomplished are reminiscent of the words of Joseph in Genesis 50:20: "Ye thought evil …God meant it unto good."
>
> p. 60

The providence of God manifested itself, not only in the protection that Moses received in the river, but with the one who found him.

Pharaoh's daughter was moved with compassion toward Moses and spared him. This is an example of God using people in a providential way to move his people to the place where he wants them. She also spoke to his sister, Miriam, who was allowed to come into the presence of Pharaoh's daughter. Consider the fact that a Hebrew girl came upon the daughter of Pharaoh and her servants as she was bathing. How could it be that a lowly Hebrew was able to gain access to such royalty? In normal circumstances it would not happen, but with God's providence, all things are possible. The girl was able to approach and suggest that she be allowed to fetch a Hebrew woman to nurse and care for the child as a service to this prominent woman. The woman that was chosen to raise the baby was his own mother. If Moses ever doubted his purpose, he need only look back to his beginning to discover that God had a plan for his life.

Moses received the best of education from two worlds; he knew of the Hebrew culture and God, and he knew of the finer education of Egypt, including military strategy and leadership skills.

As we speak of God's providence, let it not be forgotten that the hand of God was involved even when Moses rose up and slew an Egyptian, as recorded in Scripture:

> And it came to pass in those days, when Moses was grown, that he went out unto his brethren, and looked on their burdens: and he spied an Egyptian smiting a Hebrew, one of his brethren. And he looked this way and that way, and when he saw that there was no man, he slew the Egyptian, and hid him in the sand.
>
> Exodus 2:11–12 (KJV)

God allowed Moses to be moved by the plight of his people to go out and see their state and then placed him in a position to defend one of his brethren. This action forced Moses into a position where he could no longer be comfortable in Egypt, and in time, he was forced to leave. After his departure from Egypt, Moses continued the educational tract that God had set him upon. John J. Davis, in his book Moses and the Gods of Egypt, wrote:

> As Moses grew older, he would become more and more involved in formal education in Egypt …Moses was forced to leave the land of Egypt and flee eastward to the land of Midian… The long years in the desert were not wasted years, but times of further maturity and reflection in the things of God …God was preparing Moses to be a leader of men, so for forty years he received experience by leading the flocks of the Midianite priest.
>
> pp. 63–65

These are things that happened to him, for the most part. He made few decisions up to this point about the things that would shape his life.

Personality Traits

The Scriptures point out something unique about Moses that both his mother and the Pharaoh's daughter saw in him that I believe speaks to his personality or specialness. The Scriptures point out something unique about Moses in Exodus 2:2. It is recorded that "his mother saw that he was a goodly child" (KJV). A special quality that had illuminated even in infancy was seen in Moses, and the favor of God that was upon him moved others, including Pharaoh's daughter, to extend him favor.

A person will sometimes find him or herself receiving special favor and drawing the admiration of others, and within this is the unique quality of personality God uses to move a person through the graciousness of others to the place where he wants them.

Some people attend costly seminars or special classes on how to win friends and influence people, but others are just born with it. They take no special classes; they are themselves, and with that, they have many doors opened to them. To the person who experiences such, know that God has allowed his favor upon you, not for your own personal consumption, but for you to allow him to move you and use you to his glory. The person who uses this favor for personal profit and prestige will find that, in the end, they will be empty and alone. But the one who uses it for God's purposes will be rich, full, and surrounded by others who love God as well.

Another personality trait of Moses was his integrity. He could have easily kept quiet and enjoyed the luxuries of Egypt, but something moved him. John J. Davis wrote in Moses and the Gods of Egypt:

> For forty years Moses had enjoyed the privileges and prestige of a prince in Egypt. Participation in certain royal processions and enjoyment of entertainment would have been a normal part of his daily experience. The time had come, however, when one of the biggest decisions of his life had to be made

> and that related to identification. Should he remain in the royal court and enjoy all the luxuries afforded him there or cast his lot with the people of God...Whatever the influencing factor, Moses, by faith, turned his back on the opportunities and riches that could have been his and joined the Hebrews.
>
> p. 67

Moses's integrity forced him to be true to himself when he could have easily chosen otherwise. We have heard it said, "To thine own self be true," and Moses was true to himself, his people, and, most of all, his God.

God will use our integrity as a tool to move us to that place where he wants us. Have you ever been in a situation where you could have remained silent but felt compelled to speak out anyway? Have you made a choice before to stop something that you could have readily gotten away with because no one knew? This is what integrity is and what it does. Those who lack integrity lack the moral compass that has been given by God to often lead us quietly and gently to the place of his divine will. Are you listening?

Natural Abilities

The Bible speaks of Moses's strength, which he possessed even in his old age: "And Moses was an hundred and twenty years old when he died: his eye was not dim, nor his natural force abated" (Deuteronomy 34:7, KJV).

God had apparently gifted Moses with natural strength and vigor, which he maintained throughout his life. In order for him to be a leader of the people of Israel, the first they had ever known, he would need to command their attention and respect. Each child of God has been gifted with some natural ability that God desires to be used to not only bring them to the place of his will but to aid the believer in accomplishing God's desired task for the person once they find themselves where God wants them.

Moses not only had natural abilities, but he also had what may be termed a natural disability as well. Moses stated it himself:

> And Moses said unto the Lord, O my Lord, I am not eloquent, neither heretofore, nor since thou hast spoken unto thy servant, but I am slow of speech, and of a slow tongue.
>
> Exodus 4:10 (KJV)

Moses did not excel in the area of speech. It caused him great concern, and this was probably something he struggled with all of his life. He found himself content to spend the rest of his life out in the pasture with sheep that couldn't care less about a slow-tongued, mush-mouthed shepherd.

The problem Moses had was not a disability in the sense that we understand it in our modern terminology, but rather an area of his life where he realized he had shortcomings and did not shine the best. Each of us can relate to that feeling, but proof to all who may question

God's ability to use imperfect creatures is found in the fact that he used flawed Moses and accomplished great things through him. Even in his reluctance, God used this imperfect servant, and he will do the same with us. Moses had no idea what was really in him and what he was capable of accomplishing until he was challenged to act. Many men and women have discovered a hidden latent talent and ability when they were forced to act by no choice of their own. Necessity dictated the need to step up, and the rest is history. They unexpectedly began to shine in ways they could have never imagined. God wanted to do the same in Moses's life, but his fear and reluctance prohibited it. God used his brother, Aaron, as his audible mouthpiece, but the written words of Moses still ring in the ears of generations that have come along long after his death.

Urging/Calling

Moses is one of the first characters in our study that exemplified an urging or calling to serve or minister on God's behalf. We catch a glimpse of this when it is said: "And it came to pass in those days, when Moses was grown, that he went out unto his brethren, and looked on their burdens" (Exodus 2:11, KJV).

Moses felt something within him that brought him to a point of dissatisfaction with Egypt and moved him to have compassion and concern for the Israelites in their affliction. I believe God placed an urging or calling upon him. We often refer to this as a burden that God has laid upon our heart. The Apostle Paul expressed the same urging, as we will examine later in this book.

Hebrews 11:24-25 speaks of Moses growing weary with Egypt, refusing to be numbered with the house of Pharaoh or being called the son of Pharaohs' daughter and making a choice to suffer with slaves rather than enjoy the pleasures afforded a king. Maybe Moses did not even recognize himself what it was that was moving within his heart to cause him to become so disillusioned and dissatisfied with his privileged life. But God knew, and from our vantage point, we too know.

Luke records in Acts 7:23-24 how Moses, at the age of forty, made a conscious decision to defend a Hebrew slave being mistreated by an Egyptian, thus casting his lot with his Hebrew brethren. The thing that stands out most is the emphasis the Holy Spirit gives to the statement "... it came into his heart to visit his brethren the children of Israel..." What thing could have moved so powerfully within Moses as to cause him to do this thing?

Do you wonder who the impetus of the thought was? For anyone who may doubt God's ability to lay a burden upon one's heart, the evidence is now clear. I am not advocating some secret wisdom, special message, or revelation, but merely God placing a sense of need, a desire, and urgency upon the heart of his people.

As we read further in Hebrews, Moses did not reject Egypt or even flee because of mere fear or some other ulterior motive but because of a greater reward and respect for God. God spoke to his heart by placing a burden upon him that he refused to ignore.

Jephthah

Jephthah was a most unlikely choice for being selected as a judge over God's people. He was the son of a woman with a seedy lifestyle, the product of an illicit relationship, and, in time, was cast out of his father's home by his half brothers. This little bit of introduction alone is enough to suggest that his life's story would not have a happy ending. Jephthah's life should serve as encouragement to those who examine it that God is in control and he is able to take the worst of circumstances and the most rejected and dejected of society and work wonders in and through them.

Providence

God's providence showed up at the beginning of Jephthah's life, even at his conception. Though God does not lead men into sinful acts, he can take the sinful acts of men and use them to his purposes. We must remember, as we look at Jephthah's life, that providence involves God using circumstances, adversities, trials, and people to bring us to the place of his will. We can see a combination of these working together simultaneously in his life. His father is identified as a man named Gilead. Gilead met, at some point in his life on an unspecified occasion, a harlot and had a sexual encounter with her. From this relationship Jephthah was born, and through circumstances that are not explained, he is raised in Gilead's home, even while he is married and his wife is bearing him other sons. Once the other sons of Gilead were grown, they threw Jephthah out and declared to him that he had no place or inheritance in the family or house of Gilead. From our previous discussions, we remember that providence is when things happen to you that are not of your doing. Jephthah had nothing to do with his mother's life choice to be a harlot, his father's decision to have an illicit relationship, the home he was raised in, and he certainly had nothing to do with the fact that his half brothers were unkind to him. All of these things just happened to him. God's providence happens to us and is totally beyond our control. The lesson of his life is that when life appears to just happen, in reality, it is God moving us in some fashion into the place of his divine will? It is our mission to remain faithful, patient, and encouraged, knowing that "Lord, as long as I know that it is you, I can be okay and rest assured."

What could have been God's plan for his life in allowing him to be in such a situation? As students of the Scripture, we know that toughness is a characteristic that would be much needed in the life of the judges that God would use to deliver his people from their oppressors. What better way to develop toughness and strength of character than to be a prostitute's kid, to be raised in the home of the married man that impregnated your mother, and be raised in the same house with the sons of the man—did I leave out being raised by Gilead's wife, the boys' mom? Can you imagine Jephthah's life? He probably felt as if no one liked him; it was him against the world, but it was all a part of God's plan to develop a judge who would one day deliver his people from their enemies.

Another needed attribute for a judge as deliverer would be that of being a warrior. I suppose we can easily figure that Jephthah probably learned to fight and fight often early in life. The half brothers he was raised around did not seem to care much for him, and maybe others in the village felt the same. Needless to say, he may have had to deal with ridicule because of his mother's lifestyle and the circumstances around his conception and birth. These all served to prepare a warrior mentality in him that he would need later in life. He had no way of knowing that with each fight, confrontation, and verbal spar, he was being shaped to fight for Israel and lead the Israelites into victory.

Many saints spend far too much time crying about their circumstances rather than seeing the possibilities of what God may be doing. Granted, I do my fair share of crying as well, but we would all do well learning to have a different perspective as we face difficult circumstances and people. Jephthah is called "a mighty man of valor." A man of valor is a warrior, and that is exactly what was being developed through the course of his life. Surely he did not like the experiences of his life, but such is the case when God is forging us into fit instruments and moving us into place. God is described as the potter, and we are the clay. Clay has no say in its shaping and forming; it simply yields to the mighty hand of the potter.

A judge of Israel would also need to be a leader. Had Jephthah not been driven from home, he may never have become a leader. The years of hardness seemed to have developed a toughness and independence in him that attracted other men to him as someone to follow. It is said of Jephthah: "Then fled Jephthah from his brethren…and there were gathered vain men to Jephthah and went out with him" (Judges 11:3, KJV). Keil and Delitzsch note: "…Loose men gathered round him" (cf. Judges 9:4) and "went out with him, viz., upon warlike and predatory expeditions like the Bedouins" (p. 274).

Notice he did not appear to actively seek followers in order to create a band of marauders, but men of tough, rugged character appear to have been attracted to him. There was some type of leadership qualities that were readily apparent in him, and it may be attributed to his upbringing and the difficult life he endured.

Not only did Jephthah become a leader, but he also seems to have been an effective one. This is assumed because a type of fame evidently went out about him, and he developed a reputation of being a successful conqueror. His band was successful in pillaging and defeating those who they encountered. The elders of his former village called for him when they were in need of a leader, protector, and military general. The children of Ammon, an enemy of Israel, made war against them, and it was apparent that no one in Israel was up to the challenge of leading a charge against them. So a call went out for Jephthah to return home and protect his people and village. The elders actually sent a delegation to the land of Tob, where Jephthah now lived, to fetch him home. His reputation preceded him, but this time, he was not being ridiculed or rejected, but requested. They pled for him to come home, be their captain, and lead them to victory.

Personality Traits

Jephthah's hard life developed in him what are now much-needed personality traits. He had a hardnosed, no-nonsense attitude about him. This was seen in his dealings with the elders of his former village. He was driving the negotiations and had a take-no-prisoners attitude. He said, in essence, "You guys called me, and now I will set the terms," and he also had a chance to throw a little bit of sarcasm in their faces as well. As part of his argument, Jephthah said, "Did not ye hate me, and expel me out of my father's house? And why are ye come unto me now when ye are in distress?" (Judges 11:7, KJV)

Jephthah played hardball with them and made demands upon them if they were going to enlist his help. God may allow us to suffer at the hands of our enemies, but he is also able to turn the tables and cause us to see our adversaries bow before us in need and beg for our assistance. His promise to Christ was that he would make his enemies his footstool, and that is one promise we may realize as well if, when faced with adversity, we respond in the way that pleases God, "though he was reviled he reviled not."

God may want us to develop a no-nonsense attitude about some things in our lives and dealings with men, maybe to be stronger and firmer in addressing wrongs, sins, and evil actions of men. The key to knowing when

God is moving is when things happen to us. The things that befell Jephthah shaped him to stand firm on that day and others that soon followed.

In my own life, I have seen God bring difficult people and situations into my life to develop firmness, a bit of hardnosed no-nonsenseness. By nature, I am a more laid back and easy-going person, but in ministry, there are times when a stand must be taken. In such times, there will be a need to stand firm and stare down the wrong acts, intents, and attitudes of those who would harm the body of Christ. While I was going through those difficult times, I had no way of knowing that something else was coming down the pike that God wanted me to face and conquer. He will not only bring people into your life that will challenge you to develop desired traits but will also bring people who may serve as role models, support systems, and allies to face the evils that will need to be encountered. I am personally thankful for the good men and women he has brought into my life who rubbed off on me, supported me, and taught me about strength and toughness. I would like to think that they have benefited from their association with me as well.

Paul was such an example and influence in the life of a young minister by the name of Timothy. Timothy was a nice guy and somewhat timid, but as a minister, he faced many challenges with strength and resolve. As the apostle worked with him, I am sure a bit of Paul rubbed off on young Timothy, yet the old apostle constantly encouraged him to be strong, not be afraid, not let anyone intimidate him, and not let anyone look down on his youth or ministry. There were evils and inappropriate acts that Timothy needed to face and correct, and with Paul's help, we are sure that he did not fail.

Jephthah also developed a trait of being a negotiator and one who could argue and reason well. Negotiators normally have to go to school and spend countless hours in study, training, and at the side of experienced persons before they can be prepared to negotiate on behalf of nations, but there stood Jephthah, having learned to argue with reason in the halls of God's school called life or, as some have referred to it, "the school of hard knocks." John C. Davis, in A History of Israel, explains the negotiating prowess of Jephthah:

> Jephthah postulates four arguments in answer to the charge of the King of Ammon. First of all he pointed out that the land which Israel possessed was originally in the hands of the Amorites, not the Ammonites. The second argument of Jephthah was a religious argument stating that the God of Israel gave that land to Israel. The third argument of Jephthah was one based on political precedent. That Balak, an earlier Moabite king, did not fight against Israel on the grounds of land rights, then why should the king of Ammon do so this late in history? The final argument of Jephthah in the negotiations was a time argument. He pointed out that the king of Ammon had, in effect, waited too long to make claim to that territory, for

> 300 years had passed since Israel settled in Heshbon on the east side of the Jordan.
>
> pp. 123–124

We can only wonder on how many different occasions in his young life that Jephthah had to argue and defend himself against the onslaught of attacks from his family and fellow villagers. He developed skills that would serve him well later in life. He had no way of knowing that God was at work and preparing him for this day when he would present these well-reasoned and articulate arguments before the king of Ammon.

Two final personality traits emerge: devotion and loyalty. He may not have witnessed much of these qualities in his childhood; nonetheless, they developed within him. They are demonstrated by his vow to God to sacrifice whatever he had if God would be with him and give him the victory. But how could he possibly know what his words would cost him?

The person that came from his door to meet him upon his victorious return was none other than his only child, his daughter.

It is widely argued as to what Jephthah actually did in response to his vow. Jamieson, Fausset, and Brown comment and make this assertion:

> The shriek, and other accompaniments of irrepressible grief, seem to indicate that her life was to be forfeited as a sacrifice; the nature of the sacrifice (which was abhorrent to the character of God) and distance from

> the tabernacle does not suffice to overturn this view, which the language and whole strain of the narrative plainly support; and although the lapse of two months might be supposed to have afforded time for reflection, and a better sense of his duty, there is but too much reason to conclude that he was impelled to the fulfillment by the dictates of a pious but unenlightened conscience.
>
> Judges 11:34–40 (KJV)

It is difficult to know with certainty, but suffice it to say, that in some form or another, he was true to his vow. Whether she was actually sacrificed, which would be abhorrent to Jehovah, or she was dedicated to the Lord and spent the rest of her life in service to God and never married, we will never know. But Jephthah proved himself devoted and loyal to the God, who delivered him and gave him success. How much so should devotion and loyalty be as traits in the life of those who claim to walk with him today? These are possible when the believer comes to grips with the fact that God is guiding their lives and is actively involved at all times. How can one not be devoted and loyal to such a God?

Ruth

Ruth, the grandmother of King David, comes on the biblical scene after the death of her husband. She became a prominent character in scripture, and many sermons, lessons, and conversations will be spoken and proclaimed concerning her and her life for ages to come. If she were asked the question, "What is God's will for your life?" during the days she lived, she may have said, as many do, "I don't know." We are advantaged to view her life and see clearly how God moved her into the position where he wanted her.

Providence

Ruth lived in Moab and met her husband while living there. A series of events unfolded that illustrated the providence of God that was at work in her life.

If Ruth were able to speak, she would say, "I was minding my own business, and one day I met Mahlon, and from that point, everything in my life changed forever."

God uses trials and adversities as tools to work his providence in the lives of his people. Notice the text said there was a famine in the land, which necessitated the move of Naomi and Elimelech to the land of Moab. A famine! God not only uses people and circumstances, but he also uses nature for his purposes. The famine that struck their native land forced them to move in search of water, food, and a better life. Many questions come to the minds of those who have suffered during catastrophic events like hurricanes, tornados, floods, and fires. They wonder why bad things happen to good people and the innocent. But this story, which the Holy Spirit moved holy men to write, is for those who suffer. They can know that God has not abandoned them and is at work in their lives, even in the midst of tragedy.

Elimelech and Naomi carried their two adult sons, Mahlon and Chilion, with them. While in the land of Moab, these two brothers met and married Moabitish women. Mahlon married Ruth, and Chilion married Orpah. It is recorded that Naomi's husband, Elimelech, died, and in the course of time, so did her two sons, and the three anguished widows were left alone. Naomi then saw the need to return to her own country of Judah, for she had heard that "…the Lord had visited his people in giving them bread" (Ruth 1:6, KJV). The famine was over, and Naomi had no reason to continue in Moab. She and her daughters-in-law headed back to Judah, but along the way, Naomi stopped and urged them to return to their mothers' homes in their own country. Orpah returned at the urging of Naomi, but Ruth remained and committed to her mother-in-law in beautiful fashion with words that will be discussed in a subsequent section.

The two women returned to Judah and were greeted by friends and acquaintances:

> So they two went until they came to Bethlehem. And it came to pass, when they were come to Bethlehem, that all the city

> was moved about them, and they said," Is this Naomi?"
>
> Ruth 1:19 (KJV)

Naomi was at a low point in her life and felt abandoned and punished by God. Her words portray her inward feelings of hopelessness and despair as she told the people of Bethlehem and her kinsmen, "Call me not Naomi, call me Mara: for the Almighty hath dealt bitterly with me..." (Ruth 1:20-21, KJV). Her birth name, Naomi, means "pleasant," beautiful, and delightful, but the present situation was far from what those words convey. We can scarcely understand the overwhelming sense of grief and abandonment that she must have felt. Her words portray a heart that is totally empty and void of joy, and there was no beauty or anything delightful on her horizon.

Does this sound familiar from your own experiences or those of someone you know? She actually felt as if God was against her. The name Mara means bitter, and maybe she felt some bitterness inwardly. But little did she know that God would bring a wondrous thing from her misery, for the Messiah would be born to her family and rejoicing would return to her spirit in time. God has not promised to remove our hurts and negative experiences but will work his will in our lives in spite of them all, as the words of the Apostle Paul remind us: "And we know that all things work together for good to them that love God, to them who are called according to his purpose" (Romans 8:28, KJV).

Once home and settled in, they needed to survive and find food. So Naomi sent Ruth out to find a field to glean in that they may eat. God's providence is further seen by Ruth going out and randomly selecting a field to glean in and gather food for her and her mother-in-law. The field she selected belonged to a man by the name of Boaz. Here again, God moved in her life to bring her into contact with the people he would use to get her into position to be in his revealed will for her life. She did not know the field was his, but God knew, and he guided her directly to the place where he wanted her. The book that bears her name declares:

> And she went, and came, and gleaned in the field after the reapers: and her hap was to light on a part of the field belonging unto Boaz, who was of the kindred of Elimelech.
>
> Ruth 2:3 (KJV)

Some may say she was lucky or would consider it happenstance, but what appears to be a chance event from man's perspective is the providence of God. With him moving in the life of his children, there are no chance encounters, accidents, or incidents of good fortune, just his providence guiding us to the place where he wants us at any given time.

God was not done with using people as a part of his providential workings, for the nearest kinsman redeemer could have taken Ruth along with all of the possessions and property of Elimelech, but he is recorded as saying: "I cannot redeem it for myself. Lest

I mar mine own inheritance: redeem thou my right to thyself; for I cannot redeem it" (Ruth 4:6, KJV).

She had no power in choosing which kinsman she would be with, but God did, and he moved her into the arms and home of Obed. From these two would spring Jesse and, from him, King David. What an awesome God we serve, and how comforting it is to know that he moves in our lives even today.

Personality Traits

Ruth possessed a few traits that were obvious and appealing. She had an admirable quality about her that others readily saw and were attracted to. She was devoted and loyal in relationships, a worshiper of God, industrious, and virtuous.

Her attractiveness, which was not only due to her physical beauty but her inward beauty, was demonstrated upon her return to Bethlehem with Naomi. The story indicated that she was well received by the town's people partly due to her devotion and kindness to her mother-in-law. Edith Dean, in All of the Women of the Bible, wrote:

> The people of the little town of Bethlehem admired her, not because of her genius or her foresight or her great beauty, but because of her womanly sweetness. Modest, meek, courteous, loyal, responsible, gentle yet decisive, Ruth always seems to do the right thing at the right time.
>
> p. 82

History is replete with examples of men and women who possessed outward beauty and handsomeness. For many of them, the only beauty they possessed was outward, for they have displayed some of the ugliest dispositions known. The Bible speaks of those whose only beauty is that of an outward form: "As a jewel of gold in a swine's snout, so is a fair woman which is without discretion" (Proverbs 11:22, KJV).

When all a person possesses is outward, it is not long that they can be tolerated. But not so with Ruth; she had a deep, abiding beauty that attracted others and held them captive by the unseen power of a beautiful character. God used her inward beauty to gain her favor in the eyes of the people. He can and will use both inward and outward beauty found in his servants to guide them to the place of his divine will for their lives.

Ruth's devotion in relationships is highlighted in the book that bears her name. It can only be imagined that she was a devoted and loving wife to Mahlon before his death. We assume this because of her relationship and demonstrated love and devotion to Naomi, the mother of Mahlon. Few wives could have such love for their mothers-in-law and not have had the same for the son. She was so devoted to Naomi that, rather than going back to her own people and family in Moab, she made the decision to journey with Naomi to a strange land and worship a God that she had not known prior to her marriage to Mahlon. Her statement in Ruth 1:16 (KJV), "...thy people shall be my people, and thy God my God," indicates that she did not have a prior relationship with Jehovah, though she may have heard of him being a close neighbor to Judah. She was willing to be, not only devoted to Naomi, but to the God of Naomi. How commendable is the legacy of Ruth to have come to the knowledge of the God of Abraham, Isaac, and Jacob and be willing to embrace him as hers.

God ordained that any stranger who was willing to embrace him was to be embraced by his people as well and to be fairly treated. Notice God's command in relation to strangers:

> And when a stranger shall sojourn with thee, and will keep the Passover to the Lord, let all his males be circumcised, and then let him come near and keep it; and he shall be as one that is born in the land: for no uncircumcised person shall eat thereof. One law shall be to him that is homeborn, and unto the stranger that sojourneth among you.
>
> Exodus 12:48–49 (KJV)

> Love ye therefore the stranger: for ye were strangers in the land of Egypt.
>
> Deuteronomy 10:19 (KJV)

This is exactly what the people of Bethlehem did toward Ruth, as we have previously read. It is one thing to do something out of fear and in response to a command, but how much easier it is to obey God's command to love the stranger when the stranger has demonstrated such love and devotion, as that which Ruth has demonstrated. She was a devoted wife, daughter-in-law, and worshiper of God.

Ruth was industrious, which is always a cherished quality in women, as evidenced in the praise lauded by the words of King Lemuel in Proverbs 31:13–22. Ruth was not afraid to work and provide for herself and Naomi: "And Ruth the Moabitess said unto Naomi, Let me now go to the field, and glean ears of corn after him in whose sight I shall find grace" (Ruth 2:2, KJV).

When seeking God's revealed will for one's life, that person must always be sure that they are moving, working, and being industrious, as was Ruth. One story that the Lord conveys illustrates God's desire that man and woman alike be about the business of being industrious and productive: "And about the eleventh hour he went out and found others standing idle, and saith unto them, Why stand ye here all the day idle?" (Matthew 20:6, KJV).

I have found that even when I was not sure of God's will for my life or which way I should go, sitting idle was surely not the answer. It is when men and women move, get busy, and become industrious that they often discover a sense of peace about God's will for them.

It is interesting to note that once she got up and began to move and work, the assurance she sought of knowing God was guiding her became evident. It is right before us in the story of her life: "And she went, and came and gleaned in the field after the reapers: and her hap was to light on a part of the field belonging unto Boaz, who was of the kindred of Elimelech" (Ruth 2:3, KJV).

Happenstance does not exist for the children of God. God is always in control and guiding his children. Ask yourself, how did she end up gleaning in the field of Boaz, who is one of two near kinsmen in Bethlehem? Do you see how being industrious aids in discovering the will of God for your life? You can't just pray and sit on the couch and expect to hear a voice coming from the chimney. You must get up, get busy, and become industrious, and in the process, God will reveal his will for your life.

The last trait we see of Ruth is her virtuousness. Although she may have been a beautiful woman as some have stated, such as Irving Fineman's reference in All of the Women of the Bible. Edith Dean includes his estimation of Ruth's beauty: "Whose radiant beauty of face and form neither the shadows nor the sad state of her raiment could obscure" (p. 82). Ruth did not use her beauty, nor did she allow others to use her in ways that were not becoming of a woman of virtue.

The account of Naomi advising Ruth to go to the threshing floor of Boaz and lay at his feet must not be misconstrued:

> And it shall be, when he lieth down, that thou shalt mark the place where he shall lie, and thou shalt go in, and uncover his feet, and lay thee down; and he will tell thee what thou shalt do.
>
> Ruth 3:4 (KJV)

There was nothing neither lewd nor untoward in the scene. This is an apparent custom and practice of the time to signal to the near kinsman a request or desire for protection. Edith Dean comments on this process:

> The measure recommended by Naomi and adopted by Ruth was equivalent to a legal call on Boaz, as the supposed nearest kinsman of the family, to fulfill the duty of that relationship. An archaic custom this was, and one which subjected Ruth to a severe moral test, but she had confidence in her mother-in-law's judgment and she also knew that Boaz had proved himself to be meticulously upright.
>
> p. 86

Ruth demonstrated her honorable intentions in her statement to Boaz: "I am Ruth thine handmaid: spread therefore thy skirt over thine handmaid; for thou art a near kinsman" (Ruth 3:9, KJV). This indicates nothing but a desire to have Boaz fulfill his role as near kinsman. Boaz's response sums up the virtuous quality of Ruth's character: "And now, my daughter, fear not; I will do to thee all that thou requirest: for all the city of my people doth know that thou art a virtuous woman" (Ruth 3:11, KJV).

God had a purpose for Ruth's life, not only to be in the lineage of Christ, but to show all what love and devotion looked like, to touch the life of a village and an old widow to assure her that the God of her fathers still cared for her. Naomi felt bitter against God at one point and felt abandoned, but God uses people to bless people. Who knows how God wants to use us, but at least know this: he does, in fact, want to use every child of his for his glory.

Ruth's virtuous quality should stand as a lesson to those who seek to know God's will for their lives. She walked in the will of God as one who avoided actions that displeased him or brought reproach upon his name. Although God is able to bring about his will for our lives even in our disobedience, it is so much better when we walk in obedience in the same way as this virtuous woman named Ruth.

Samuel

Samuel can be appropriately named the "son born of prayer," who heard the voice of God in the night hours and became priest and counselor to kings. Samuel now comes before us to show how God has a will and purpose for every child of his.

Providence

If ever the providence of God was seen in Scripture, the story of Samuel's conception, birth, and eventual place in Israelite leadership should serve as one of the chief stories. His mother, Hannah, was barren, heartbroken, and vexed by a rival wife. She cried before God because of her troubled spirit and was heard by him.

Within the providence of God, the twin companions, trial and adversity, often appear. Hannah's trial and inability to bear children was proof of God's divine will for her life and that of her yet unborn child. Be reminded that when we suffer adversity for righteousness' sake or for reasons unknown, God is working and moving. He even uses the unpleasant things of life to accomplish his will. Consider this: had Hannah not had to pour out her heart in anguish for this child, she may not have dedicated him to the Lord as she did. Then there would be no Samuel, who stands so prominently in the Scripture as does the child that she labored for in prayer.

She was so troubled that on one special day, a prayer she uttered was transcribed and forever captured in the pages of inspiration by the Holy Spirit:

> And she was in bitterness of soul, and prayed unto the Lord, and wept sore. And she vowed a vow, and said, O Lord of host, if thou wilt indeed look on the affliction of thine handmaid, and remember me, and not forget thine handmaid, but wilt give unto thine handmaid a man child, then I will give him unto the Lord all the days of his life, and there shall no razor come upon his head.
>
> 1 Samuel 1:10–11 (KJV)

Long before his birth, his destiny was established. His mother purposed that he would be a man wholly dedicated to the service of God for all of his life.

Adam Clarke views this dedicatory prayer as going a step further:

> Samuel, as a descendant of the house of Levi, was the Lord's property from twenty-five years of age till fifty; but the vow here implies that he should be consecrated to the Lord from his infancy to his death, and that he should not only act as a Levite, but as a Nazarite, on whose head no razor should pass.
>
> p. 207

Samuel was unique in that he was dedicated to begin his service as a child under the tutelage of an old priest named Eli.

Here we find a child yet unborn on whose life the hand of God was moving providentially. I am reminded of God's word to another prophet: "Before I formed thee in the belly, I knew thee; and before thou camest forth out of the womb I sanctified thee, and ordained thee a prophet unto the nations" (Jeremiah 1:5, KJV).

As a believer, I am comforted by such words and reminded that he holds me and all others in the palms of his hands. God's providence and assurance that he has all things under control as it relates to the lives of all men, especially his people, should move men to bow before him in reverent awe and with obedient hearts.

As discussed earlier, Hannah was hard in prayer, and the Bible says that God heard her and remembered her: "...and the Lord remembered her" (1 Samuel 1:19, KJV). She conceived, bore a son, and named him Samuel, which means "asked of God." Hannah was true to her word, and after the boy was weaned, she delivered him to the man of God, as promised. Up to that point, Samuel had no choices in what would happen in his life, but all the while, God was moving and making decisions that would place young Samuel right where God wanted him. The Bible says he began his service before the Lord, along with the priest Eli: "But Samuel ministered before the Lord, being a child, girded with a linen ephod; and the child Samuel ministered unto the Lord before Eli" (Samuel 2:18, 3:1, KJV).

Once the boy Samuel was in the house of Eli, God began to immediately move and start using the child as his vessel: The text says something interesting: "The word of the Lord was precious in those days; there was no open vision" (1 Samuel 3:1, KJV).

Samuel possessed a quality that appeared lacking in his day, but this aspect will be explored in greater detail later in the section on personality traits. Let us note some details of God's using Samuel in the arena of providence and revelation.

As the Lord spoke to the child in the night, he revealed his providential work that would be performed in the life of Samuel's mentor, Eli, and his household. Eli had been too lenient and his sons far too disobedient, and God's judgment loomed in the near future. I am sure that the circumstance Samuel found himself in had a lasting impact upon him. He was used by God to convey to Eli that because of the wickedness of his sons and Eli's failure to restrain them, judgment was coming upon his house.

A comment on Samuel's witnessing the sinful acts of Eli's house is recorded in Great People of the Bible and How they Lived:

> During his early years at the Temple, Samuel was a firsthand witness to the corruption and decadence that had come to characterize the priesthood at Shiloh. The worst offenders were Eli's sons, Hophni and Phinehas. They habitually stole food brought by pilgrims as offerings for sacrifice, cooked it contrary

> to sacrificial law, seduced women who had come to worship there and otherwise profaned their priestly roles.
>
> p. 136

Consider the revelation of God to the child of what he was about to do to Eli's household. What impact do you suppose that had upon this lad? From this, I believe he learned to take God and his work seriously. He knew of the love and faithfulness of God, but he had also heard of the wrath of God upon those who transgressed against his will and made a mockery of holy things.

This may even be a glimpse into Samuel's reaction to Saul, who would later play the same game of transgression and mockery: "And Samuel said, What meaneth then this bleating of the sheep in mine ears, and the lowing of the oxen which I hear?" (1 Samuel 15:14, KJV) Samuel had little toleration for those who blatantly disregarded the will of God and mocked those things that were holy.

God's providence in Samuel's life eventually became evident to all of Israel. It is said: "And Samuel grew and the Lord was with him, and did let none of his words fall to the ground..." (1 Samuel 3:19-20, KJV). Samuel's position as God's approved prophet was made known throughout all Israel, and the land knew without a doubt he was God's man.

The Interpreter's Bible expounds on this and says:

> To the Israelite a word was an almost concrete expression of the character and inten-

> tions of the person who uttered it, and partook of that character and those intentions. Like men, words could be either active (Hebrews 4:12) or idle (Matthew 12:36). The active ones do what they say; they accomplish that which the speaker pleases (Isaiah 55:10–11). The idle ones fall to the ground and do nothing. The word of the Lord is active; he speaks and it is done (Psalm 33:6, 9), and since the words which Samuel spoke were the words of the Lord, the Lord was continually watching over his word to perform it (Jeremiah 1:12). The result was that whatever Samuel said came true" (1 Samuel 9:6).
>
> p. 896

Samuel witnessed the providence of God on one occasion, which was totally unrelated to himself, but I believe it had a lasting impact upon him. After the Philistines vanquished Israel in battle and had taken the ark of God into their coasts, God began to bring judgment upon them until they returned the ark to Israel. Samuel beheld how God brought plagues upon the Philistines until they were moved to send the ark back to Israel. Samuel was so impressed by the event that he recorded the account as the Philistines were preparing to send the ark back:

> Now therefore make a new cart, and take two milch kine, on which there hath come no yoke, and tie the kine to the cart, and bring their calves home from them: And take the

> ark of the Lord, and lay it upon the cart … and see if it goeth up by the way of his own coast to Beth-shemesh, then he (God) hath done us this great evil: but if not, then we shall know that it is not his hand that smote us: it was a chance that happened to us. And the men did so; and took the two milch kine, and tied them to the cart, and shut up their calves at home …And the kine took the straight way to the way of Beth-shemesh, and went along the highway, lowing as they went, and turned not aside to the right hand or to the left.
>
> 1 Samuel 6:7–12 (KJV)

How marvelous a sight it must have been to see these two animals moving against all natural instinct to deliver the ark of God back to the people of Israel.

As Samuel learned on that day, God can use even the natural world to show his people his providential will. I'm sure Samuel marked this in his mind. I wonder if any of us who call on God's name have taken the time to notice if God is using something in the natural world to tell us something of his will for our lives.

God also extends his divine favor upon his people in an effort to accomplish the task of moving us to the place of his will. Just as God gave favor to Moses, so he does with Samuel. He establishes him as his approved prophet providentially by allowing all of the words that Samuel spoke to come to pass. An examination of one's life may reveal how God may have moved in some similar fashion to approve the person as being from God. The working of God in the life of his modern-day servant does not have to be on the grand scale as those of biblical heroes, but by merely serving and blessing others, they reflect the favor of God that is upon them. Some of you have had people say how much of a blessing you have been to them in their lives. They don't just say it to be nice but can recount specific actions or words that blessed them in specific and tangible ways. The difference between people being nice and complimentary as opposed to expressing real benefits from being touched by God's servants is often the ability to cite specific words, details, and events that have been spoken and done that have had an impact.

Passion

Samuel expressed a passion for the things of God by the way he responded to the evil actions of the people of his day. He was grieved when men turned from the Lord and felt a personal sense of rejection as they rejected God and his commands.

Samuel urged the people to repent in 1 Samuel 7:3; he cried unto the Lord on Israel's behalf in 1 Samuel 7:9, and it is said, "God heard him." He was grieved by Israel's rejection of God as they clamored for a king in order to be like their neighboring nations. He even felt a personal rejection by their rejection of God as their theocratic head in 1 Samuel 8:5–7.

In 1 Samuel 12:3, Samuel recounted his righteous life as a testimony of his faithful service. He chastised Saul for foolishly taking on a priestly function of offering up a sacrifice. He confronted Saul for his disobedience of not totally destroying Amalek and its King Agag but brought him and his possessions back as spoils of war. Samuel's famous quote reverberates thousands of years later:

> Hath the Lord as great delight in burnt offerings and sacrifice, as in obeying the voice of the Lord? Behold, to obey is better than sacrifice, and to harken than the fat of rams.
>
> 1 Samuel 15:22 (KJV)

Samuel's passion for God was demonstrated by his completion of the task that Saul had been commanded: the annihilation of Agag and the Amalekites, as recorded in 1 Samuel 15:33. Passion is not merely an emotion, but it is evidenced by devotion, obedience, and action. Samuel proved his passion by fulfilling the will of God.

God gives us passion for various things, and when we are able to identify our passion and channel it to the glory of God, we are then moving closer and closer to the place that he has for us.

Personality Traits

Two personality traits stand out with Samuel: sensitivity to the voice and things of God and faithfulness.

I have found in my time as a minister (sorry, guys!) that it appears women tend to have a greater sensitivity to the things of God. Churches are mainly full of women, your greatest church workers are normally women, and countless mothers serve as the spiritual leaders in their homes. The home of the young evangelist Timothy was no different. The Apostle Paul spoke of Timothy's faith, which had its origin in that of his grandmother Lois and mother Eunice. These women transmitted their faith to young Timothy by their example of devotion, steadfastness, service, and trust in the Lord Jesus. Paul does not present himself in scripture as someone who was easily impressed. He was a Pharisee of Pharisees, as he stated concerning himself, and did not show much patience for those who were weak and skittish in their faith. His dispute with Barnabas over John Mark's departure from the mission field appears to demonstrate Paul's lack of tolerance for those who could not stand up to the arduous work of ministry. So for him to state Timothy's faithfulness means a great deal. Paul even said of Timothy, "I have no man like-minded" (Philippians 2:20, KJV). Paul's words of praise for Timothy's mother and grandmother in establishing faith in the young man shows how he recognized the spiritual sensitivity of women and their key roles in the spiritual nurturing of children.

Samuel's spirituality and focus came from his mother. In the time she had with him before he was sent to live with Eli, she helped him drink deeply from the cup of faith, spirituality, and devotion to God. This early training set the stage for a heart that was sensitive to the voice and things of God. This sensitivity was shown early on in his life. Once he was at the Temple with Eli, he began to experience encounters with God but was completely unaware of who he was.

At this point, we need to go back and examine a statement from scripture: "And the word of the Lord was precious in those days; there was no open vision" (1 Samuel 3:1, KJV).

Adam Clark commented on this statement:

> There were but few revelations from God; and therefore because the word was scarce, therefore it was valuable…There was no public accredited prophet; one with whom the secret of the Lord was known to dwell.
>
> p. 216

The Interpreter's Bible sheds light as well: "Communications from God such as that described in this chapter were so infrequent that Samuel at once gained fame as a prophet" (p. 892).

Samuel was rare, and, because of his sensitivity, God spoke to him and revealed his planned work and judgment upon the house of Eli.

The sensitivity of Samuel and God's choice of speaking to him and accrediting him as his prophet conveys meaning for today's believer. I'm not advocating that having sensitivity to God today will cause him to speak audibly, but he speaks through his Word to all who are willing to hear. The Hebrew writer declared: "God, who at sundry times and in diverse manners spake in times past unto the fathers by the prophets, hath in these last days spoken unto us by his son" (Hebrews 1:1–2, KJV).

A positive personality trait for all who call on his name is that of being sensitive to the voice of God and to the things of God. I have met people who go to church and do church stuff, but their hearts are not sensitive to God or the things that concern him.

One may ask, "How is this done?" By simply allowing your heart to be touched by that which is read and heard from the Scriptures when rightly divided. Eli told Samuel what to say the next time he heard the voice of God: "Speak, Lord, for thy servant heareth" (1 Samuel 3:9, KJV). God is not in the business of forcing any one of his children to do anything; he merely speaks, and we must willfully obey. Jesus was famous for saying, "He that hath ears to hear let him hear" (Mark 4:9, KJV).

How many times has God spoken yet we refused to hear? On the other hand, we made ourselves willfully ignorant in order to assuage our conscience. This is a dangerous maneuver, for in time, if we choose not to hear, God will stop talking or allow us to believe the lies we have chosen. May we who look to God for guidance forever have hearts that are sensitive to his voice and to the things he cares about. This will always ensure that we are being moved to the place where God wants us, as was Samuel.

Samuel was also a faithful servant of God. His early years of training and education, no doubt, played a key role in his development of a faithful characteristic. It would have been easy for him to be slack and faithless, as he had plenty of examples before him in the persons of Eli's evil sons. But the child Samuel took a different turn in his walk before God.

The Apostle Paul spoke of the need for faithfulness in the life of God's servants: "Moreover it is required in stewards, that a man be found faithful" (1 Corinthians 4:2, KJV). Since the beginning of time, God has sought out faithful servants who would uphold his standards and stand against the evils of the world. Samuel was such a person. He stood firm and on God's side, even when those who had been charged with the responsibility of being a guide to the people failed. He declared God's word to the old priest, even as he stood before his mentor as a child. He stood before the people and urged repentance upon them. He stood face-to-face with King Saul and chastised him for his disobedience. He brought God's judgment upon King Agag. He rebuked King Saul yet again when Saul went to the witch of Endor and summoned him from the grave for counsel. At every turn in his life, Samuel proved himself faithful to God no matter who or what the opposition.

Samuel was particularly disturbed about an occasion of faithlessness on the part of Israel, as recorded in the book that bears his name:

> Then all the elders of Israel gathered themselves together, and came to Samuel unto Ramah, and said unto him, Behold, thou art old, and thy sons walk not in thy ways: now make us a king to judge us like all the nations. But the thing displeased Samuel, when they said; Give us a king to judge us. And Samuel prayed unto the Lord.
>
> 1 Samuel 8:4–6 (KJV)

He remained faithful to the end of his life, and because of this, he was able to stand before the people and speak words that every servant should strive to utter:

> I am old and gray headed …Behold, here I am: witness against me before the Lord, and before his anointed: whose ox have I taken? Or whose ass have I taken? Or whom have I defrauded? Whom have I oppressed or of whose hand have I received any bribe to blind mine eyes therewith? …The Lord is witness against you, and his anointed is witness this day, that ye have not found aught in my hand. And they answered, He is witness.
>
> 1 Samuel 12:2–5 (KJV)

When the child of God demonstrates such faithfulness, it will be a small thing for God to lead him to the place of his will.

David

David can be called "the shepherd boy who would be king." To every kid and parent, be assured that God has a plan for you and for your child. He took a rugged little kid who spent his days leading sheep and transformed him into a leader of a nation.

Providence

David is one of the rare characters in our study that will have all five of the indicators that were mentioned earlier in this book. He was moved by providence, exhibited passion, his personality reflected God's leading, he possessed natural abilities, and he demonstrated a calling and urging to step forward in service to God.

There are times when the providence of God is revealed as he moves one person off the scene to make room for his chosen vessel. Long before David was aware of the workings of God in preparing him to be king, God was in the process of removing Saul as king.

Saul was told on two different occasions by Samuel that God would take the kingdom from him and give it to another:

> But now thy kingdom shall not continue: the Lord hath sought him a man after his own heart.
>
> 1 Samuel 13:14 (KJV)

> The Lord hath rent the kingdom of Israel from thee this day, and hath given it to a neighbor of thine, that is better than thee.
>
> 1 Samuel 15:28 (KJV)

While Saul reigned, he demonstrated a disregard for the will of God, and for this, he lost his kingdom. In his place, God was moving to prepare the next king who would sit upon the throne.

To prepare the next king, God used trials and circumstances to develop this "man after his own heart." We are not able to pinpoint the date of this encounter, but we are told of something that happened in the life of a boy who was tending to his father's sheep. The boy's name was David, and he rehearsed this instance to Saul and the army of Israel as they faced a formidable enemy:

> And David said unto Saul, Thy servant kept his father's sheep, and there came a lion, and a bear, and took a lamb out of the flock: And I went out after him, and smote him and delivered it out of his mouth: and when he arose against me, I caught him by his beard, and smote him, and slew him.
>
> 1 Samuel 17:34–35 (KJV)

David had no way of knowing that this encounter was preparing him to face an enemy that put fear into the hearts of hardened men of war and even in the heart of a king. Believers need to learn from David that those daily, mundane battles that are encountered and won are preparing the saint for a greater battle and placing them in a position for victory. Had he not experienced the delivering power of God when he faced the lion and the bear, he too would have trembled before the giant called Goliath.

Most Christians cringe when they face battles, trials, and tests, but be not afraid, beloved; the battles are only designed to prepare you for something greater and to increase your faith in the power of Almighty God.

David faced even more trials and enemies after his defeat of Goliath, including king and mentor, King Saul. Even during these times, David had to lean upon God and welcome the people that God would bring into his life to aid him. This aid came in the unique relationship he shared with his adversary's son, Jonathan. David developed a close relationship with Jonathan, so much so that it is said their souls were knit together; they loved one another as they loved their own souls, and they agreed to enter into a covenant relationship with one another. God brought these two young men together to form an alliance, which proved beneficial to both parties. David realized early on in their relationship the value of the friendship covenant, while it would not be until much later that Jonathan benefited, although it would after his death.

The Lord has blessed my life with people who providentially crossed my path. Some passed by briefly, while others lingered much longer. My wife told me of an occasion when she was stranded because the car she was driving broke down on an exit ramp. Because I was at work, she called my mother for help because she was much closer. Once she arrived, neither of them knew what to do but lifted up the hood to check out what it might be while the car was still in the roadway without any emergency flashers on. Out of nowhere she retells, a man appeared walking toward them and yelling for them to get out of the street and away from the traffic. He helped them to push the car to a safe place and went on his way without accepting anything for the aid that he rendered. She calls him an angel from God because he delivered the two ladies from a perilous situation.

At another time in my life, while in ministerial school, I was befriended by a brother in Christ, a man who was old enough to be my father who blessed me and my family in those days of financial struggle for a starving student. He had his own home repair business and allowed me to work with him on some weekends. Believe me when I tell you that I bent more nails than I drove, and yet he paid me well. The pay was not for work rendered but an act of kindness and generosity. He has since gone on from this life to the next, but I will always be thankful for this brother in the Lord. Whether for a brief period or extended, they have each blessed me beyond anything that I deserved, and for these people, I am forever thankful to my heavenly Father.

Sometimes Christians will unwittingly reject the aid that God may send in the form of other people. God uses people to bless and aid his children, and we must overcome the independent, go-it-alone attitude that is characteristic of some. The Hebrew writer encouraged brotherly love and hospitality with these words: "Be not forgetful to entertain strangers: for thereby some have entertained angels unawares" (Hebrews 13:2, KJV). This message is not only about the need to be hospitable but about God's plan to use others in our lives.

Another person God used that had a major impact upon David's life was Nathan the prophet. He provided guidance and leveled a charge against him that shocked the foundation of David's life and also saved his soul. Nathan posed a scenario to David of an injustice committed at the hands of a rich man against a poor man. Upon hearing of the story, David was enraged and said such a man should die. Then Nathan spoke words that have been restated millions of times by those who handle the word of God, "Thou art the man" (2 Samuel 12:7, KJV).

God's use of Nathan served to shake David to his core, and it helped deliver him from a path of sin that would have led to his demise. The amazing providence of God as he uses people in the life of his children is simply amazing. Thank you, Father, for using people as your tools to shape us, convict us, and move us to be the people that you desire for us to be and moving us to the place you have for us. How are you viewing the people God brings into your life? Whether they are good or bad, God uses people for our ultimate good.

Passion

David had a passion for God—as a man, that is rare—and we should give thanks to God that the Holy Spirit has recorded it for our posterity. My wish is that more men would adopt such a spirit. One of his famous psalms speaks of his passion: "For the zeal of thine house hath eaten me up…" (Psalm 69:9, KJV). A look at his life shows the passion he had for God.

Even before we actually met David, God declared the boy's passion and heart, "…the Lord hath sought him a man after his own heart…" (1 Samuel 13:14, KJV). Adam Clark commented about the meaning of being a man after God's own heart:

> In what sense was David a man after God's own heart?
>
> 1. In his strict attention to the law and worship of God.
> 2. In his admitting, the whole of his conduct, that God was king in Israel, and that he himself was but his vicegerent.
> 3. In his never attempting to alter any of those laws, or in the least change the Israelitish constitution.
> 4. In all his public official conduct he acted according to the Divine mind, and fulfilled the will of his Maker.
>
> p. 248

He was passionate about the things of God.

As David penned many of the psalms, his passion spilled forth. They are too numerous to point out, but a quick reading will reveal his passion, time and time again, throughout the psalms.

David's passion was also seen in his defiance before Goliath. King Saul feared, Israel's army feared, but not David. Hear now the words of this passionate boy in the face of a great enemy: "Let no man's heart fail because of him; thy servant will go and fight with this Philistine" (1 Samuel 17:32, KJV).

The only way to explain such a statement is to say the person is either foolish or passionate about the cause for which they stand, and truly we know that this young man was by no means foolish.

A final act of passion on David's part that we shall discuss was his desire to build a temple for the Lord. A day came when he rested in his palace after God had given him victory over his enemies that David spoke these words: "See now, I dwell in a house of cedar, but the ark of God dwelleth within curtains" (1 Samuel 7:2, KJV).

David's comments are further expanded in another book:

> And David said to Solomon his son, as for me, it was in my mind to build a house unto the name of the Lord my God. But the word of the Lord came to me, saying, Thou hast shed blood abundantly, and hast made great wars: thou shalt not build a house unto my name, because thou hast shed much blood upon the earth in my sight.
>
> 1 Chronicles 22:7–8 (KJV)

David wanted badly to build a house to the name of God but was not allowed to do so. Yet God promised him that his son would do so, and history confirms that Solomon did indeed build the first temple to house the ark of God. God uses all things to move his children;

even their passions will be tools to get them where he wants them.

Maybe a self-examination of your own passions would be of help in discovering what it is that God wants for your life and where he wants you so that he may use you as a choice vessel and fit instrument.

Natural Abilities

David was gifted with several natural abilities or qualities that served him well and has been a source of tremendous comfort to generations long after his death.

The Bible says that David was a handsome young man: "Now he was ruddy, and withal of a beautiful countenance, and goodly to look to" (1 Samuel 16:12, KJV). Like it or not, it seems that beauty has always had its advantages. True enough, David's attractiveness was not the reason that he was chosen by God, for he himself said "…For the Lord seeth not as man seeth; for man looketh on the outward appearance, but the Lord looketh on the heart" (1 Samuel 16:7, KJV). Nevertheless, David's attractiveness was highlighted by the Holy Spirit for a reason. David not only needed to appeal to God, which is by the heart; he needed also to appeal to the people, which is far too often by the external. David's handsomeness is discussed by Robert Alter in The David Story: "And he was ruddy, with fine eyes and goodly to look on…David's good looks will play a crucial role in the magnetic effect he is to have on women and men" (pg. 97).

God, for reasons that we cannot comprehend, has chosen to use many beautiful people in his service. The

Scriptures speak of Joseph's and Moses's goodly appearance and Sarah's and Ruth's beauty. Saul, David, and Solomon are described as handsome men. This is by no means an indictment against those who have not been blessed with physical attractiveness or those deemed as average, but the correlation cannot be denied. David's physical beauty is a natural quality that God used to bring him to the place of his divine will.

Let me explain why his beauty is vital. The first king chosen by God was handsome:

> And he had a son, whose name was Saul, a choice young man, and a goodly: and there was not among the children of Israel a goodlier person than he: from his shoulders and upward he was higher than any of the people.
>
> 1 Samuel 9:2 (KJV)

David was chosen, and the same quality was attributed to him. I believe that although God looks at the heart, he understood that man's limited focus would only allow the masses to see the external. The first three kings of Israel were all said to be handsome men. The people were shortsighted and saw only the outside. For this reason, God wanted men who would win the hearts of the people in order for them to lead the people before Almighty God. Quite possibly, a man of average attraction or one who would be considered unattractive may not have been able to win the hearts of the people.

What does this say to people in this time? God indeed sees the heart, and we should never be as shortsighted as the people before whom the kings of Israel stood. But physical beauty can be a tool God uses to move his children to the place where he wants them to accomplish his will. Beauty opens doors that otherwise may not be open; that is a reality. Maybe God has gifted you with physical beauty, not for your own conceit, but to allow you to be in a place to be a blessing to his people and to the world.

The reality of life is that not everyone will be beautiful and highly attractive. With this in mind, here's a word to those who are considered average: Beauty is skin deep; it does not guarantee success or God's favor. Saul, in all of his beauty, was a failure. Nothing is directly said of the Son of Man's appearance, but Isaiah's words proclaim, "…and when we shall see him, there is no beauty that we should desire him" (Isaiah 53:2, KJV). Though his physical appearance is not described, he was, however, a resounding success and one of the most attractive (inwardly) persons to ever walk the earth. Jesus attracted men, women, and children with his inward beauty and character. The average person can still attract people with their beauty and character and point them to the Father.

David's physical nature is emphasized as well. If David were alive today, he would be termed as a physical and athletic-type person. He was rugged and "outdoorsy," as we say. David fought with a lion and a bear as a child and was not squeamish about getting into a fray. This athletic, physically active characteristic would serve him well prior to and during his reign. David's brother, Eliab, recognized his desire to see and be a part of a good fight when he said: "I know thy pride, and the haughtiness of thine heart; for thou art come down that thou mightiest see the battle" (Samuel 17:28, KJV). You've just got to love a kid like this; he was scrappy and unafraid.

His outdoor and active nature helped him to develop a skill that proved invaluable: David perfected the art of the slingshot. Adam Clarke commented on the lethality of the sling once its use is perfected: "In the use of the sling it requires much practice to hit the mark; but when once this dexterity is acquired, the sling is nearly as fatal as the musket or bow" (pp. 264-265).

Over the course of time, David had perfected his use of the sling. Possibly many days had been spent in target practice, knocking off old pottery or throwing at some field rodent. His slingshot became an extension of his arm, and he used it with deadly accuracy.

On the biggest day of his life, David stood face-to-face with a giant of a man. Armed with only a staff, a slingshot, and the unseen power of God, he leveled the mighty warrior and won the victory.

How little do we know that the small, seemingly mundane, and insignificant talents and abilities we have may be called upon to serve God or men in a powerful way. David's lesson says to all who call upon the name of God: do not discount your abilities, no matter how small or obscure they may seem.

The final natural ability we shall examine of David is his musical skills. David played the lyre and played it well. He not only played music but wrote songs and melodies as well. Countless numbers of people have found refuge, comfort, and hope in the many psalms that are attributed to David.

There are many talented people within the body of Christ who fear to use their God-given skills. There could well be someone in need of being blessed by what you may have to offer. Consider how empty the Scriptures would be were it not for David, who through the art of song, illuminated hearts and strengthened weak and feeble knees.

Personality Traits

David's personality is seen in his bravery, childlike faith, humility, kind and loving spirit, and spiritual sensitivity.

He is presented as fearless in his encounters with wild animals, views of battles and wars, and his own skirmish with Goliath. His personality, as a boy, was a reckless one that emboldened him to run headlong in the face of danger. In the midst of his fearlessness, he was not truly one who was reckless, but one who had a childlike faith in God. David referenced that he was not running in his own strength but moving on faith in what God was able to do in the face of impossible situations, David said, moreover, "The Lord that delivered me out of the paw of the lion, and out of the paw of the bear, he will deliver me out of the hand of this Philistine" (1 Samuel 17:37, KJV). It was not foolishness but faithfulness that moved David.

David displayed humility before the people and King Saul: "And David behaved himself wisely in all his ways; and the Lord was with him" (1 Samuel 18:14,

KJV). Even as Saul attempted to lure him into marrying his daughter, David saw himself as not worthy: "Who am I? And what is my life, or my father's family in Israel, that I should be son-in-law to the king?" (1 Samuel 18:18, KJV)

Saul tried to use the people to inflate David's ego, but it failed because of his true humility:

> And Saul commanded his servants, saying, Commune with David secretly, and say, Behold, the king hath delight in thee, and all his servants love thee: now therefore be the king's son-in-law. And Saul's servants spake those words in the ears of David. And David said, Seemeth it to you a light thing to be a king's son-in-law, seeing that I am a poor man, and lightly esteemed?
>
> 1 Samuel 18:22–23 (KJV)

Weaker men would have caved in to such enticements, but not David. He would not yield until he had proven himself and was able to pay the dowry that Saul eventually stated for his daughter's hand in marriage.

The record says that Saul turned against David and pursued him to take his life, and even with that, David was a different kind of man. His humility was genuine even to the point that when occasions arose that gave him opportunity to slay Saul, David would not do so: "The Lord forbid that I should do this thing unto my master, the Lord's anointed, to stretch forth mine hand against him, seeing he is the anointed of the Lord" (1 Samuel 24:6,10; 26:9, 11, 23, KJV).

David's finest hour in relation to humility came after his darkest hours. He penned Psalm 51 as a statement of his submission and repentance before God. Listen to the tone of humility from these passages, which space does not permit to be written in entirety. But as you read the full text, it screams of humility and brokenness: "Have mercy upon me, O God…The sacrifices of God are a broken spirit: a broken and a contrite heart…" (Psalm 51:1–17, KJV).

Although he was gifted in so many areas, he fell prey to the same problem that plagues all of humanity: sin. The only remedy for sin is a heart of humility before Almighty God; then and only then can God use you and bring you to the place of his divine will.

Urging/Calling

I believe David felt a calling. His questioning of his brothers and other soldiers leads me to believe this. When he sensed the fear that filled the army of Israel, this calling led him to inquire about Goliath and the king's ransom for the man who defeated Israel's enemy. His words to Saul, recounting how God had delivered him from the lion and the bear and would deliver him from the Philistine, say, "I'm the man for this hour!"

David declared God's calling and intervention in the life of every man as he spoke in the Psalms:

> O Lord, thou hast searched me, and known me. Thou knowest my downsitting and mine uprising, thou understandest my thought afar off…

> Thou hast beset me behind and before, and laid thine hand upon me.
>
> Psalm 139:1–5 (KJV)

How could he not feel a calling upon his life when he acknowledged that God directs our paths as his people from the beginning to the end?

David also felt a calling to build a house for God, as previously discussed, but because of his bloodshed in war, he was not allowed to do so. Yet God blessed him for his desire and allowed his son, Solomon, to build the house that David himself longed to build in honor of his God.

David's life is a wonderful lesson of the hand of God being upon the life of those who love him. He was known as a man after God's own heart. We can look back with clarity and see the movements of God in his life, but are we paying attention to his movements in our own lives? He is still the shepherd that leads beside the still waters; let him lead you.

Abigail

Abigail was an obscure woman who suffered silently in the same house with a foolish husband. Others would view her life as a loss and doomed, but the God that moves in the lives of his people saw something completely different.

As she bursts on the scene, it is easy for the Bible reader to develop sympathy for Abigail. Her plight is that of having made for her the poor choice of being married to one of the worst men in the Bible, Nabal. But it is from her life that a wealth of encouragement comes for those who walk the earth today. Her life says, "God is still in control, he sees your situation, understands, is sympathetic, and will deliver you in his own way and in his own time."

Providence

Providence will show up in Abigail's life in the form of circumstances, people, and trials. This is often the way God's providence will show up in every person's life.

The first act of providence is circumstances. Samuel's death was the occasion that the whole nation of Israel mourned. It was on this occasion that David, after his participation in the burial procession, made a journey to the wilderness of Paran. While there, he came upon the herds of a wealthy man, and his presence provided protection for the man's herd and laborers. The wealthy man's name was Nabal, and, had Samuel not died,

David may well not have found himself in the place where he stood. God uses circumstances, like a perfect storm, to bring people and things together to aid in accomplishing his will.

Most Christians overlook day-to-day circumstances and, in doing so, miss the working of God in their lives. The saying, "Not seeing the forest for the trees," is appropriate in the lives of most. It is so easy to get caught up in living and experiencing life that we can miss the impact that circumstances play in how God works and moves in our lives. Circumstances are situations that come to you or that you find yourself in without your input or doing. When you hire on to a new job, there is no way of knowing whom you will meet and develop relationships with.

On one occasion in my own life, a circumstance happened that I ignored until God revealed it to me. I was in the military and received orders while stationed in Germany that my new base would be in South Carolina. I did not want to go to South Carolina, rather California or Hawaii. Seeing that Uncle Sam did not ask me about it, I knew that all I could do was obey, so South Carolina here I come.

Once there, I began to meet some wonderful people and found a church that was exciting and refreshing with two godly men who served as ministers. Under their instructions, I began to develop a hunger for ministry and a passion for the things of God more so than ever before in my life. God had begun this process in my life long ago, but now things were moving up a notch. It was not long before I became the youth minister and then met the woman who would become my bride. Now, after twenty-five years of marriage and ministry, we both look back and see the movement of God in bringing me to South Carolina. It was there that the preaching bug bit me, and even though there may be peaches in Georgia, I found my own precious fruit (Joyce Capers Jones) in a small town called Sumter, South Carolina.

Abigail found herself in somewhat the same situation. She was minding her own business, just trying to survive a miserable marriage to a foolish man. The scripture showers her with praise and compliments about her character, grace, and beauty: "…she was a woman of good understanding and a beautiful countenance" (1 Samuel 25:3, KJV). We are not told of the circumstances that led to such a beautiful and kind woman being married to such a terrible man, but it may have been an arranged marriage by her parents, which again she had no choice in the matter.

No matter what our circumstances, be assured that God is aware of it, has permitted it, and will deliver us or empower us to endure in his own time. Abigail's deliverance came as David was moved into her life by the hand of God.

The next act of providence was people. David appeared in her life as she rushed to deliver her house from certain death. David had provided protection to the sheepherders of Nabal and, as was custom, asked for compensation for his kind act toward Nabal's servants and the protection of his possessions. Nabal, being true to character, rejected David's request, insulted him, and shamefully dismissed the service that had been provided. Abigail moved with haste upon hearing from one of her servants what had transpired between her husband and David and of David's intentions. Little did she know that this man would soon be her husband instead of Nabal.

She had not set out to meet David; providence brought their paths together because God had determined to bring deliverance into the life of this kind and good woman.

The third act of providence is trials. Abigail was in the midst of a trial that she had not created, but her evil husband, in his foolish act, had placed a death sentence upon her whole household. In anger, David proclaimed that all of Nabal's house would be destroyed and his possessions taken:

> Now David had said, Surely in vain have I kept all that this fellow hath in the wilderness, so that nothing was missed of all that pertained unto him: and he hath requitted me evil for good. So and more also do God unto the enemies of David, if I leave of all that pertain to him by the morning light any that pisseth against the wall.
>
> 1 Samuel 25:21–22 (KJV)

It is said that she ran to meet David and pled for the lives of her family and household. She offered gifts to him and made him aware of the fact that she was not aware of the exchange and request.

One can only imagine the fear that gripped her heart upon hearing of David's intentions. So many lives were at stake: her life, her servants, her husband, and any children that were in the home. What a weight of responsibility and trial to find herself facing. She moved wisely and did what was right by interceding on behalf of her house and seeking to make amends for her husband's foolishness.

Her trial is the impetus that moved her to meet with David and make her plea. Trials can be used by God to move us to places that he has designated for us at various times in our lives. At that hour, she needed to be before David to save lives and make an impression that David would not soon forget. Trials are not comfortable, enjoyable, or desired, but they are used by God to move his children into position for blessings and greater works that he desires to accomplish in their lives.

Personality Traits

Abigail is noted for her good understanding. It was this good understanding that allowed her to move rightly in sparing her household from the sword of David and his men. The Holy Spirit made a contrast between the poor character of Nabal and the understanding character of Abigail. She appears to have had a positive relationship with her servants as well, as one of them came running to her to inform her of the intentions of David in response to her husband's evil treatment.

Later, after Nabal's death, her personality shows again. She could have had visions of grandeur in being married to David, but she was willing to assume a servant's role and give her attention to the needs of others. David dispatched his men to fetch Abigail to be his wife, and her response spoke volumes about her character: "And she arose, and bowed herself on her face to the earth, and said, 'Behold, let thine handmaid be a servant to wash the feet of the servants of my Lord'" (1 Samuel 25:41, KJV). Remember, this was a wealthy woman that was being asked to be wife to David. She was used to having servants tend to her, not the other way around. Yet she was humble enough to say that she was willing to wash the feet of David's servants.

It may be a stretch, but I believe that Abigail was a person who may have regularly treated her own servants with kindness and found ways to even serve them and make their lives better as they were in her employment in the household of Nabal. People don't just become a person of her character overnight; it is in them and has been a part of them for many years.

I am convinced that David witnessed something in Abigail that caught his attention on that day when she interceded for her house—something that he never forgot. This same something caused him to call for her after her husband's death:

> And when David heard that Nabal was dead, he said, Blessed be the Lord, that hath pleaded the cause of my reproach from the hand of Nabal, and hath kept his servant from evil, for the Lord hath returned the wickedness of Nabal upon his own head. And

> David sent and communed with Abigail, to take him to wife.
>
> 1 Samuel 25:39 (KJV)

A wife such as Abigail was sure to have a positive influence in the life of David for years to come. She was described by Edith Dean as "humble and gentile, while David was described as willful and tempestuous" (p. 105). Her positive personality traits would indeed be a blessing to the man who would reign as king of Israel. It is interesting to note that Nabal profited little from the influence of his wife, while on the other hand, in one brief encounter, David had already profited from her influence. It was her words of entreaty that turned David's wrath from destroying her household and sparing many innocent lives. Who among us can know how powerful our God-given personality traits may influence another person in profound ways? Remember the words of Christ, "Ye are the salt of the earth..." (Matthew 5:13, KJV), as you move among people and, by your personality, influence them for good.

God used her beautiful personality to open a door of deliverance from her miserable situation. When he opens such doors, we must be wise enough to see and move with haste. I love the way the story closes: "And Abigail hasted, and arose, and rode...and she went after the messengers of David, and became his wife" (1 Samuel 25: 42, KJV). She did not waste time; she got up and hit the door that God had opened, and I'm sure she never looked back.

Amos

Amos, a common man who herded sheep and gathered sycamore fruit for a living, was guided by God to be one of his most outspoken prophets. Who could have seen being a prophet and God's spokesperson on the horizon for him?

Providence

Not much is recorded about the personal life of Amos, but the Bible reader can draw lessons from the obvious life and trials that a man of his day would face, particularly a herdsman. The providential hand of God moved in this servant's life and is an assurance to us that he still moves even today.

As a herdsman of sheep, Amos roamed the rugged terrain of the region of Tekoa. It is recorded that the terrain was rugged and uninviting, which would prove to be a testing and training ground for the prophet. God will send his people to some of the most uninviting places to prepare them for his work and will. Amos's training ground is best described by Homer Hailey:

> Across this wilderness swept the hot winds of the south; and from its hills could be heard the roar of the lion, the cry of the jackal, and the bleating of sheep as their sounds echoed from one canyon wall to the other. It was here that the prophet had grown up as a

> "herdsman of sheep" and "a dresser of sycamore-trees." This environment had prepared him well for the stern task to which he was called and is reflected most colorfully in the prophet's preaching.
>
> p. 82

The God we serve must not be misunderstood as he moves us into harsh environments because they may only be our proving and training grounds. The providence of God is not guaranteed to yield a comfortable situation but will always yield fruit if we are patient and obedient.

Passion

Amos's passion bleeds through in his preaching and condemnation of the various groups identified in his book. It seems that God calls men and women to serve most often in areas where there is a natural passion within them that makes them most fit for the task at hand.

As a herdsman, he was a man of compassion and patience. He witnessed death as some of his sheep were lost to the beasts of the field and surely felt indignation when the strong took advantage of the weak. God channeled this indignation and formed a strong defender of the poor. The passion that burns within the heart of a child of God is used by God to move them into the place where they may best serve. Amos lived among the poor and served among the weak and defenseless. This would serve him well as he would later be called to declare God's judgment to the mighty and powerful exploiters of the weak and defenseless.

Personality Traits

Amos's traits of courage, strong character, devotion to God, patience, and tenderness flow throughout his book. He needed courage as he stood before kings, such as Uzziah and Jeroboam, and as he pronounced God's judgment upon Damascus, Gaza, Tyre, Edom, Ammon, and Moab.

Courage and strength of character were two important traits that were most needed. Any man or woman who desires to understand God's will for their lives need only look at certain personality traits that are God-given to lend clues as to where the Lord would have them to be and what he would have them to do. Amos's traits send a clear message that he was born to confront sin and injustices, for only a strong backbone would suffice for this task.

He was also devoted to God and his truths; this proved important because many of the religious and political leaders of his day had sold their souls for the luxuries of their day and for the acceptance of the powerful and the refined.

His tenderness and patience was not seen for his powerful and wicked contemporaries but for the poor and the weak. He cried out as he was moved by God. What came from the prophet may have been inspired by God, but I believe there was an inherent quality of courage within him from which this message also sprang. The reader can hear the prophet's raspy voice as he proclaimed with power and passion these words:

> Thus saith the Lord; For three transgressions of Israel, and for four, I will not turn away

> the punishment thereof; because they sold the righteous for silver, and the poor for a pair of shoes.
>
> Amos 2:6 (KJV)

For everyone who desires to know God's will for their lives, understand this: the basic ingredients for what he has called you to be or do are inherent within you. What is it that is deep down within you and spills out or even cries out without being forced? Listen to it, and move with it, for it will lead you to the work and place that he has for you.

Urging/Calling

God had a special calling for Amos. He was a simple man; there was no fanfare or anything assuming about him. God does not work the way we often think. As we look for the polished professional, the trained and refined orator, God looks at qualities far different. What God desires is not so much for us to be polished, though that has its place, but God looks for willing and obedient servants. This man who becomes God's great prophet, champion of the poor and oppressed, arose from very humble beginnings. Amos says it best when he described how he was called by God:

> I was no prophet, neither was I a prophet's son: but I was an herdsman, and a gatherer of sycamore fruit: And the Lord took me as I followed the flock, and the Lord said unto me, Go, prophesy unto my people Israel.
>
> Amos 7:14–15 (KJV)

Well, we can be assured that our calling will not be as dramatic as Amos's, but we can be assured that as Amos was called, so are we. The problem we are faced with is knowing when we have been called and to what we have been called to do. The secret is in being able to listen closely as God speaks to our hearts or uses other people to speak to us. Now let me clarify my statement: When God speaks to us, there will not be any still voices in the night that will be audible but an urging or burden that we feel to do a particular thing. Have you ever felt an urging or burden to visit a sick member or call upon another person, only to discover how vital your visit or call was to the person? That was God's call or urging for you to act. Many who are in a quandary about God's will for their lives ignore the regular call of God or fail to recognize it even as it happens repeatedly in the course of their lives.

Amos received a clear clarion call to go and prophesy to Israel, and when he received his call, he simply put down his shepherd's staff and his fruit basket and went as he had been called. As he was called, he included in his prophetic message those elements of his past experiences and incorporated them into his mission. In his book, he spoke using terms that related to a shepherd, and in chapter 8:1–2, he spoke of a basket of summer fruit which relates to his days of being a gatherer of sycamore fruit. When we are called by God, we will incorporate our past experiences into the ministry and work that he has for us.

Summary

God has provided a tapestry of characters who, through the movement of God in their lives, give us hope and an assurance. The hope and assurance that we have is that as he moved to reveal his will for their lives, he will do the same for us. The Apostle Paul said: "For whatsoever things were written aforetime were written for our learning, that we through patience and comfort of the scripture might have hope" (Romans 15:4, KJV).

What he did in the lives of these eight characters reveals how he works to move his people to the place of his divine will. We will not be privileged to have direct revelation as they did, but in subtle ways, he is still speaking clearly. We must learn to listen and know his will.

God speaks and reveals his will though providence; the means of this providence may be trials, adversities, and circumstances, whether good or bad. Providence is also carried out through the medium of other people that God allows us to cross paths with. Just as Joseph found himself in Egypt and eventually in prison, it wasn't by chance, but the will of God. For had he never been in jail, he would not have met the chief butler and, in turn, the pharaoh, which led to his promotion and the salvation of his people.

God's will for us can also be revealed by the passion that is within us. Every person has a passion for something, and that passion may be an indicator of God's will for one's life. Whatever drives you can also be the thing that God wants to use to bless the kingdom and the world. Some people may never have allowed themselves to get in touch with their passion because people often suppress who they are in favor of being what others may want them to be.

The New Testament said something key about Christ, which allowed him to use his passion to fulfill the will of God. John recorded a statement as the scene of the last Passover meal unfolded: "Jesus knowing that the Father had given all things into his hands, and that he was come from God, and went to God" (John 13:3, KJV).

He knew who he was, and when we know who we are, we are able to realize our passion and move with confidence. This knowing caused Christ to have an unparalleled passion, as recorded by John: "...The zeal of thine house hath eaten me up" (John 2:17, KJV) and earlier Christ said, "...I must be about my Father's business" (Luke 2:49, KJV). Knowing who you are and realizing your passion will do much for discovering the will of God for your life.

Personality traits can be used by God to reveal how he may want to use us. As long as the trait is not something improper or un-Christlike, it may be used to move or aid us in accomplishing God's will. Some personalities are strong and stern, like Amos, which is helpful when having to confront sin or injustices that need to be addressed in the midst of an unrepentant people.

Natural abilities are another means God uses to help us understand how he may want to use us. When we have been gifted by God, we must understand that the gift is for a purpose. God desires to be glorified in his people. Paul said, "Now there are diversities of gifts, but the same Spirit" (1 Corinthians 12:4, KJV). He has gifted each saint so that the body may be edified and he may be glorified in the church and in the world.

An urging or calling is placed upon all of God's saints. Some have been called to preach the gospel—not a message in the night, but a burden upon the heart to preach. Others may have a burden for prison ministry or working among the sick. All of these signal a work or ministry that God is calling us to do. When we feel such a burden or calling, we should know that God is moving us into the place of his divine will.

All of these are used by God, but it is up to his saints to learn to look closely, sit quietly, or move upon the urging in their hearts. This will help to avoid the desperation or despondency felt by many who ask, "What does God want me to do, what is his will for my life?"

Before we move into the second section of this book, let's take time to familiarize ourselves with an inspiring example of God's quiet movements in the lives of his people. David was engaged in battle against the Philistines after becoming king of Israel. He looked for confirmation of God's will and divine assistance before advancing on the enemy. The Lord instructed him to go around to the rear of the enemy and wait until he heard a special sound, which would indicate the start of the battle. Once the sound had been heard, then he would know that the Lord had gone ahead of him to fight the battle, thus giving him the victory. Listen to God's assurance that his movements can be heard by his people to assure them of his guidance and victory:

> David inquired of the Lord and he answered, "Do not go straight up, but circle around behind them and attack them in front of the balsam trees. As soon as you hear the sound of marching in the top of the balsam trees, move quickly, because that will mean the Lord has gone out in front of you to strike the Philistine army."
>
> 2 Samuel 5:23–24 (KJV)

The question may be asked, how can I know God's will for my life? I encourage you to listen for a rustling in the treetops. God's angelic army would tread ever so lightly upon the treetops, but God instructed his servant to listen closely, and he would know that God has indeed come to the aid of his people. We can have comfort in knowing God's will for our lives if we would take the time to listen closely and block out the many distractions that hinder this process. An easy way to phrase this listening process would be to call it "listening for a rustling in the treetops." Are you listening?

Section Two: A Practical Guide for Application

It's All a Fog to Me!

One day, a young woman went about her usual routine, but there was something a little different. She was mechanical in her motions; she had no joy, no life or vigor. She had come to a point of hopelessness and despair; she was tired—tired of life and her seemingly pointlessness existence.

Is this it? she thought. Is this all there is? That evening as she lay across her bed, she cried out to God, "Lord, if you have something for me, please show me or else just take me away from here!"

On another day, in a different place, a young student nearing completion of college ponders, Lord, what am I going to do? Where do you want me? What career should I choose? He sees before him a sea of choices and paths and does not know which way to go. He loves God, has prepared himself, and now is at a crossroad. The family is steering him toward a lucrative and prestigious career, but he is conflicted and does not know exactly what to do with his life and education. He has heard all of his life that God has a will and plan for every person's life, but now he stands and wonders, How can I know what God wants me to do?

A mother is in transition; her children are all in school now, and she has lots of time on her hands and feels no longer needed since the children are older. She knows she is useful, but what should she do? She talks to her husband, family, and friends. She even talks to her minister, and, of course, he has many suggestions for helping with church matters, but what is she to do at this point in her life?

These scenarios are repeated on a grand scale throughout the world. Millions of people are finding themselves full of questions about the direction of their lives and have no clear answer. Some, unfortunately, fall into harmful habits and lifestyles in an effort to fill this void, which causes their lives to have no meaning or purpose.

Somehow these do not represent the full and abundant life that Jesus promises: "I am come that that they might have life, and that they might have it more abundantly" (John 10:10, KJV). Jesus's promise is not one of health, wealth, and fame but of purpose and meaning. He has come to give meaning and purpose to our lives. We go to his Word to learn of how to have that life which is in him. We must further learn how that abundant life is lived out in day-to-day life, not just in the great by and by. Since he has given such a promise, it stands to reason that he would give assistance to all who believe in him so that they may obtain and experience the abundant life.

There is an old saying: "He who aims at nothing invariably hits it!" The problem with most people is that they are living without paying attention to the markers that should serve to guide them to the abundant life. It is like driving in a heavy fog, looking up is of no help; turning the lights on brighter doesn't help. It is only when the lights are dimmed and close attention is paid to the road markings that the path begins to emerge.

Too many saints are like this driver who cannot see, yet they strain and look to brighter lights to help them. If they would only settle down, sit quietly, and reflect upon the subtle indicators that have already been revealed by God, they would see the path God has chosen for them.

Whenever I encounter people who want to know what God's will for their lives is, I ask them a few questions, such as: What do you like doing? What do you have a passion for? What are you gifted at? What circumstances have happened in your life that you had no control over which led to you being in a particular place or job? Questions like these are helpful in discovering God's will for our lives. Also, other people may say to you that they see a certain gift or quality in you. When this is repeated by different people that you encounter, maybe God is trying to tell you something.

The Scriptures teach us that God cares for us: "Casting all your cares upon him; for he careth for you" (1 Peter 5:7, KJV). If we believe this, then why is it that so many saints are frustrated and feel as if they are doomed to walk aimlessly through life never knowing God's will for their lives? On one occasion, the question was asked, "What wilt thou have me to do?" (Acts 9:6, KJV). God did not reveal it directly but told this servant to go to a certain city and it would be told to him what to do.

God uses other people, as he did then, to tell us what he may want us to do. As stated previously, when a consistent message is given by others that a quality, gift, or calling is seen in your life, take heed—God is trying to tell you something.

There are reasons why some saints find it difficult to see that God has a plan for them. They have been bombarded with so many negative messages that they cannot fathom being used by God for glorious purposes. Overcoming such streams of negative messages can be a chore, but the responsibility is upon the saint to do so. No one will stand before the great God of heaven and say, "They told me that I couldn't, so I didn't" and expect heaven to be satisfied.

Practical steps:

1. Pray for revelation and guidance.

   The honest seeker of God's will would do well to go to God in prayer and ask him to reveal his will for their life. "Lord! Help me to see what you want me to do or be." "If any of you lack wisdom, let him ask of God, that giveth to all men liberally, and upbraideth not; and it shall be given him" (James 1:5, KJV).

2. Get to know yourself.

   Take time to be alone with yourself and know who you are. At this point, lay aside the expectations of others and find out who you are. Be true to your own urging, calling, and desires as it relates to your talents and abilities that may be used by God. This may require a day or so of being alone and journaling your thoughts about yourself in order to draw a picture of who God made you to be.

3. Listen to what others are saying.

   This is not in conflict with the previous point but works in conjunction. The person must first know himself, and then the consistent comments of others may reveal something obvious that was overlooked in our personal observation. God saw something in Moses that he did not see in himself, and we know that God sees all and knows us best. We can, for whatever reason, overlook something that may be obvious to others.

4. Review what has happened or is happening to you.

   Circumstance is when things happen to you. God will use circumstances to move you to the place of his divine will. A review of the circumstances of our lives may reveal a picture of where God is leading. Use a journal as you do this to make note of circumstances that have occurred in your life, where they have taken you, what changes they brought, what people they allowed to cross your path, and from this a picture will emerge. You may be pleasantly surprised how God has used circumstances, good or bad, to lead you to where he wants you to be.

5. Try it; it just might work.

   Don't be afraid to labor or serve in the area that your work has led you. Trying will reveal to you if you were correct or if you need to continue to review your research until you have discovered God's will for your life. How do you know that it is right? You will know when you are successful at it, when people are blessed by it, and when the kingdom is enriched by it. These criteria will let you know that you are where God wants you. You won't have to force the emotion and passion; you won't have to solicit praise from others to keep you energized. The passion will flow naturally, and the energy will well up from within you as it did with Joseph. Whatever he put his hands to prospered because God was with him, and this was evident to Potiphar and Pharaoh.

6. Stay in touch with heaven (home base).

   Following these suggested steps will aid the saint in discovering the will of God for their own lives. As previously stated, no man can claim to know the definitive will of God. Yet as we have examined the lives of Old Testament characters, we are able to see how God was moving them to the place and position where he wanted them. The indicators we can see in their lives can be clues for us as well. Hopefully every believer will take heart and look at their life to see the handy work of Almighty God.

In the process of discovering the will of God for your life, it would serve the saint well to stop periodically and pray about where they are and to always ask for God's guidance. There are at least two important scriptures that come to mind that I feel will aid the saint in being sure to always stay in touch with heaven to be sure that their steps are in line with the will of God. The psalmist said: "Order my steps in thy word: and let not any iniquity have dominion over me" (Psalm 119:133, KJV); "The steps of a good man are ordered by the Lord: and he delighteth in his way" (Psalm 37:23, KJV).

Even the task of driving a vehicle requires constant minor adjustments in order to maintain a straight path and to stay on the road. The same is true with our being in the will of God. Just because we are doing one thing this year does not guarantee that it is the same thing that God has for us two years from now, so we always ask for his will and for guidance to do his will. At one point in his life, God needed David to tend his father's sheep, but later he needed him to be a warrior and defender of his people. Later God called David to be king, and yet later still, he was called upon to be a prolific writer to leave words of comfort, assurance, and hope for generations to come.

Staying in touch with heaven is vital. It assures that we are always seeking his will and not ours. It assures that we are in the place or doing the work that he has for us at this time.

Staying in touch with heaven requires a prayerful attitude. Paul urged believers to pray without ceasing, to always have an attitude and mind of prayer. Even the Son of man was in constant communication with heaven, and in this, he found strength to do what he had been called to do. He found encouragement when no one else understood or was able to offer what he needed, and he found hope that all would be okay as he approached the cross. The scene of the garden of Gethsemane illustrates this. Here, Christ was troubled and his soul heavy as the cross loomed. He was prepared and more than willing to do the Father's will, yet his humanity needed some things that the disciples could not give. The disciples could not provide him the support of prayer, for they were weak. They could not give him the strength to face the cross, and they could not give him the reassurance and hope of what lay beyond the cross. But God showed up and provided what was needed, even in the midst of his son's prayer: "And there appeared an angel unto him from heaven, strengthening him" (Luke 22:43, KJV).

Stay in touch with heaven. God will guide you, strengthen you, support you, and give you hope to persevere.

A Purpose for Outsiders

As I am writing this book, it is my hope that all saints would read it, be blessed, and receive assurance that God has a design and will for their lives. I am also aware that some readers who do not know Christ will read these pages and wonder, What about me? Does he have anything for me? For that reason, I include the next three topics: "A Purpose for Outsiders," "Getting on the Right Team," and "Created for Glory."

The Bible clearly teaches that God desires all men be saved and come to a saving knowledge of the Lord. But even before a man comes to Christ, God can still have a purpose for him, but the ultimate purpose is to be saved and honor God through a Christlike life.

The Bible tells us of a few individuals who were not people of God, not in the family of God or Christ, yet they were used by God. The lives of the pharaoh of the Exodus; Cyrus, the king of Persia; and Cornelius present truths that may cause others who do not know God in a covenant relationship to pause and realize that God has something in store for them as well.

There are four things that I have identified in Scripture from the accounts of the lives of these three individuals. These four things are what God seeks to accomplish through such people and one of them is what he desires to do in their lives if they would humble themselves and heed his call. I believe the facts show that God, first of all, desires to be magnified even through non-believers. Secondly, that he uses them to teach, train, prepare, and equip his people to do his will. Third, that he blesses his people and others through them. Fourth, that he desires to save them, if they would humbly submit and respond to his loving call.

The pharaoh of the Exodus account who resisted God's and Moses's pleas, but then later freed the Israelites, is a case study for how God uses unbelievers to accomplish his will. Though totally unaware of it, he was being used by God to bring honor to himself. Moses recorded God's statement concerning Pharaoh:

> And I, behold, will harden the hearts of the Egyptians, and they shall follow them: and I will get me honor upon Pharaoh, and upon all his host, upon his chariots, and upon his horsemen. And the Egyptians shall know that I am the Lord, when I have gotten me honor upon Pharaoh, upon his chariots, and upon his horsemen.
>
> Exodus 14:17–18 (KJV)

But even before Pharaoh came to this point, God had already determined that he would be made known, glorified, and honored among the Egyptians: "And the Egyptians shall know that I am the Lord, when I stretch forth mine hand upon Egypt, and bring out the children of Israel from among them" (Exodus 7:5, KJV).

God uses non-believers to bring honor to himself. The Hebrew word for honor, kabad, in this text means "to be heavy, be weighty, be honorable." God declared that he would receive honor, value, and glory through and in the eyes of the Egyptians. That which is heavy is deemed as having value, such as gold, which is of great weight and value. Pharaoh and Egypt soon discovered how heavy, valuable, and worthy of honor was the God of Israel.

The honor that God sought did not have to come in the fashion that it did. Had Pharaoh heeded Moses's initial request to let the Israelites go, God would have still been honored and magnified. Paul echoed this truth: "…For this same purpose have I raised thee up, that I might show my power in thee, and that my name might be declared throughout all the earth" (Romans 9:17, KJV).

Egypt and Pharaoh served another purpose for God and his people. They became trainers and a training ground for both Moses and the children of Israel. Egypt was initially a haven for Israel as Jacob, his sons, and their families moved there because of the great famine in the land. They received the choice land of Goshen as their portion and the favor of the pharaoh during the days of Joseph. They grew and prospered in the incubator of Egypt. They had no fear of enemies who would harass them for many years, which allowed them to grow in number and prosper until there arose another pharaoh who knew not Joseph.

The years of hardship in Egypt taught them to look to God for deliverance and to depend upon him. They learned of war and organization from the Egyptians, which prepared them for the conquest of Canaan.

Moses also learned many things while in Egypt. He studied in the schools of Egypt, was reared in Pharaoh's house, and learned military strategies and organizational skills. He was refined, knew the roles of statesmen, and had the ability to dialogue with kings. But even before that, he learned of the God of the Hebrews while he was a small child being raised by his mother as a duty to the daughter of Pharaoh. He learned the best of both worlds, and when he was of age, he chose to suffer with his brethren rather than enjoy the pleasures of Egypt for a season.

The Egyptians were a blessing to the Israelites as they were leaving Egypt. They were so eager to see them leave that they gave freely of their jewels, precious metals, livestock, and personal possessions. The Bible says that in doing so, the Israelites spoiled the Egyptians. These jewels and precious metals that were freely given would later be used to fashion items related to the tabernacle and the ark of the covenant (Exodus 25:1–35:29). Where else would the Israelites get such fine things to give as a freewill offering to the Lord for the building of his house? God has a use for nonbelievers. He often uses them to bless his children and equip them to be able to serve and worship him as the example the ancient King Cyrus's actions will show.

Our second example is King Cyrus of Persia. Long before he was born, he was prophesied to be an instrument used by God for judgment and deliverance.

> Thus saith the Lord to his anointed, to Cyrus, whose right hand I have held, to subdue nations before him; and I will lose the loins of kings, to open before him the two

> leaved gates; and the gates shall not be shut …I have raised him up in righteousness, and I will direct all his ways: he shall build my city, and he shall let go my captives, not for price nor reward, saith the Lord of host.
>
> Isaiah 45:1, 13 (KJV)

Cyrus was used as a vessel by God to bring honor to himself. Isaiah recorded that God would use this king, although he himself did not know the God of heaven: "I have even called thee by thy name: I have surnamed thee, though thou hast not known me" (Isaiah 45:4, KJV). This may be troubling to some to think of God using a non-believer to accomplish his purposes, but remember the words of the Apostle Paul:

> Even for this same purpose have I raised thee up, that I might show my power in thee, and that my name might be declared throughout all the earth. Therefore hath he mercy on whom he will have mercy, and whom he will he hardeneth…Hath not the potter power over the clay of the same lump to make one vessel unto honor, and another unto dishonor?
>
> Romans 9:17–21 (KJV)

Let this message ring loud and clear to all who read these words: God has a plan and will for your life! He may desire to use you for a specific purpose at this season in your life, but know for sure that his ultimate plan and desire is that you might be saved. There is no record of Cyrus becoming a proselyte to Judaism or trusting in the God of the Hebrews, and what a pity for such a choice vessel to only be used for a moment and then discarded for eternity all because he trusted not in the Lord.

God used this king to punish the nations who did not know him and to deliver the captives of Judah so that they may return and rebuild the city of Jerusalem. God's use of Cyrus to punish Babylon is recorded by the prophet Jeremiah:

> And it shall come to pass, when seventy years are accomplished, that I will punish the king of Babylon, and that nation, saith the Lord, for their iniquity, and the land of the Chaldeans, and will make it perpetual desolations.
>
> Jeremiah 25:12 (KJV)

The Bible, as well as recorded history, chronicles how King Cyrus granted permission to the Jews to return to their homeland. He also supplied them with provisions to resettle and rebuild their cities. The books of 2 Chronicles 36:23 and Ezra record Cyrus's decree:

> Now in the first year of Cyrus king of Persia, that the word of the Lord by the mouth of Jeremiah might be fulfilled, the Lord stirred up the spirit of Cyrus king of Persia, that he made a proclamation throughout all his

> kingdom, and put it also in writing, saying, Thus saith Cyrus king of Persia, The Lord God of heaven hath given me all kingdoms of the earth; and he hath charged me to build him a house at Jerusalem, which is in Judah. Who is there among you of all his people? his God be with him, and let him go up to Jerusalem, which is in Judah, and build the house of the Lord God of Israel, (he is the God,) which is in Jerusalem. And whosoever remaineth in any place where he sojourneth, let the men of his place help him with silver, and with gold, and with goods, and with beasts, besides the freewill offering for the house of God that is in Jerusalem.
>
> Ezra 1:1–4 (KJV)

It is intriguing to see the mighty hand of God as he uses those who do not know him in a covenant relationship to help his covenant people. This instance in Ezra is reminiscent of the Exodus from Egypt when God spoiled the Egyptians and loaded Israel down with the possessions of their former captors (Exodus 12:33-36). The same thing happens here, as those who chose to leave Persia left loaded down with the possessions of their former captors.

Our third and final example is Cornelius. Luke recorded:

> Cornelius, a centurion of the band called the Italian band, A devout man, and one that

> feared God with all his house, which gave much alms to the people, and prayed to God always.
>
> Acts 10:1–2 (KJV)

Notice something about Cornelius. He was devout and feared God with his entire house. Here was a man who was not in covenant relationship with God yet was being honored in his life. God desires to be honored by all. This may be misunderstood by some, and it may appear that God is in need of man's adulation, but this is far from the truth. Remember that God is self-sufficient and needs nothing from man. Honoring God actually does more for man than it could ever do for God. When God is honored by men, men are then walking in the will of God, which means that many of the harmful and destructive acts he may otherwise be engaged in are being avoided; thus man is the beneficiary of honoring God.

The Lord was held in high regard by Cornelius, as evidenced by his worship, respect for God, giving of alms, and continual prayers. God responds to any man's honest respect, worship, and faithfulness, as demonstrated in the life of Cornelius. Let me clarify with this caution that this does not mean those individuals are saved but that God takes note of their honoring him. Luke recorded that because of Cornelius's life, something special was said by God concerning him:

> He saw in a vision evidently, about the ninth hour of the day, an angel of God coming in

> to him, and saying unto him, "Cornelius." And when he looked on him, he was afraid, and said, "What is it, lord?" And he said unto him, "Thy prayers and thine alms are come up for a memorial before God."
>
> Acts 10:3–4 (KJV)

It is not said that he was saved but that because of his God-fearing attitude, God took notice of him, and it caused God to remember something. What did God remember? I believe that the next verse gives an indication of what was remembered: "And now send men to Joppa, and call for one Simon, whose surname is Peter" (Acts 10:5, KJV).

Cornelius's prayers and acts brought back to God's attention his promise of salvation and blessings to all men, both Jew and Gentile. In the next breath, Cornelius was told what to do in order to be saved and brought into covenant relationship with God.

The hope all men have is that God longs to be in a covenant relationship with them and will move and work in their lives to bring them to that point. Peter said it best concerning God's view of those who are outside of the family of God but whose hearts are tender and receptive to the things of God and his voice: "Of a truth I perceive that God is no respecter of persons: But in every nation he that feareth him, and worketh righteousness, is accepted with him" (Acts 10:34–35, KJV).

Getting on the Right Team

It is impossible to enjoy the benefits or the spoils of victory without being on the right team or in the right organization. Imagine a man wandering into the ceremony for the awarding of Super Bowl rings to the winner of the big game having not been a member of the team. He wouldn't get far before realization would set in with the help of security escorting him out in a not-so-kind manner to be sure.

The blessing of knowing God's will and understanding his purpose for our lives is especially reserved for his children. But for those standing on the outside looking in, there is hope. God has a plan for the salvation of all men, and he has made it plain and simple for all to understand and obey.

The Bible tells us it is God's will that all men be saved, as expressed by the Apostle Paul in his letter to Timothy: "Who will have all men to be saved and to come unto the knowledge of the truth" (1 Timothy 2:4, KJV). We must then look to the Bible to discover what is said about salvation in order to experience his saving grace. Once we are in his family, we can have the peace of knowing that he is guiding our lives and leading us to the place of his revealed will.

Our journey toward salvation starts with a simple message: "For God so loved the world that he gave his only begotten Son, that whosoever believeth in him should not perish, but have everlasting life" (John 3:16, KJV).

Yes, it is that simple; just believe in him. The idea of belief in Christ leading to salvation is not fully understood in twenty-first century terms because Christ is so much more known than in John's and Paul's day, so it is important to put this in context. When John spoke these words, there were many who had never heard of Jesus Christ and had no idea who he was. Paul elaborated more extensively on the subject later in the Roman epistle when he referenced Isaiah 28:28 in Romans 10:11, which says: "For the scripture saith, Whosoever believeth on him shall not be ashamed" (Isaiah 28:28, KJV).

Further down in the same text, he said:

> For whosoever shall call upon the name of the Lord shall be saved. How then shall they call upon him in whom they have not believed? And how shall they believe in him of whom they have not heard? And how shall they hear without a preacher (teacher)?
>
> Romans 10:11 (KJV)

Salvation is not accomplished by merely crying out a name—even the precious name of Christ Jesus—but by being taught of Christ.

The prophet Jeremiah spoke of the coming of a new covenant and made a definite distinction of a component of the old covenant and the new. In the old covenant, a person was born into the family of God, just by virtue of physical birth. Being born of Jewish ancestry made a person a child of God, and then they were taught about Jehovah. Notice God's instructions to Moses for the children of Israel:

> And these words, which I command thee this day, shall be in thine heart: And thou shalt teach them diligently unto thy children, and shalt talk of them when thou sittest in thine house, and when thou walkest by the way, and when thou liest down, and when thou risest up.
>
> Deuteronomy 6:6–7 (KJV)

But in the new covenant, a person must first be taught of God before he/she can be born of God. It is also understood that some could become a proselyte of the Jewish faith by making a decision to adopt the Jewish customs and obedience to the Law of Moses. Now listen to the words of Jeremiah:

> And they shall teach no more every man his neighbor, and every man his brother, saying, Know the Lord: for they shall all know me, from the least of them unto the greatest of them, saith the Lord.
>
> Jeremiah 31:34 (KJV)

Teaching is important in the salvation process. Even Christ made this plain in his own words: "It is written in the prophets, And they shall be all taught of God.

Every man therefore that hath heard, and hath learned of the Father, cometh unto me" (John 6:45, KJV).

Jesus gave instructions to his disciples after his resurrection, which included a command to teach all nations:

> Go ye therefore and teach all nations, baptizing them in the name of the Father, and of the Son, and of the Holy Ghost: Teaching them to observe all things whatsoever I have commanded you.
>
> Matthew 28:19–20 (KJV)

The day of Pentecost after the resurrection of Christ was a special day and a grand day. On this day, there was an outpouring of the Holy Spirit and the first gospel sermon was presented by the apostles, with Peter leading the way. In his message to a host that were gathered together, many who had never heard of Christ, he declared the truth about Jesus Christ, the Son of God. As his message drew to a close, many were convinced by what they had heard and cried out seeking the mercy of God. Listen to Peter's response to their cry and the remedy he offered to address their sin and guilt:

> Then Peter said unto them, Repent, and be baptized every one of you in the name of Jesus Christ for the remission of sins, and ye shall receive the gift of the Holy Ghost.
>
> Acts 2:38 (KJV)

To be saved, one must be taught about Christ and submit to the will of God, calling upon him in humble submission. Once a person is in the family of God, there can be a peace that has never been known before and an assurance that he will lead you to the place of his revealed will.

Created for Glory

For anyone who may be wondering why it is important to understand and know God's will for their lives, here is the answer: Until we are able to understand God's will for our lives, we will forever walk aimlessly through life, grasping after various things, trying to find meaning. I believe a proper understanding of God's will is rooted in knowing why we were created. Isaiah said that we were created for God's glory, but, unfortunately, many are not experiencing a life that glorifies God. In the beginning, God created man and gave him a work or purpose: "And the Lord God took the man, and put him into the Garden of Eden to dress it and keep it" (Genesis 2:15, KJV).

Man was made to work in whatever situation or place that God may have placed him. I'm sure at this point, someone may be asking, "What does this have to do with God's will for my life?" It has much to do with it in that unless we are willing to roll up our sleeves and work diligently in whatever situation or place God has placed us for the present, we will never realize his will for us in the long run. We need to know that God is not always the one who has put us in the place or situation that we may find ourselves, yet we must faithfully work. No matter how we got there, by God's hand or our own doing, just work until he moves you.

Although everything was prepared for Adam, he was still given a challenge to work and maintain things while he was there. God knew he would not stay in the garden, but for that time period, he had to work. Even after the fall and expulsion, man still worked in his newfound situation. Others are recorded in the Bible that was called to work while in their present situation as God was moving them along to the place of his will. There are other people whose present situation was not their destiny, yet they worked where they were until God was ready to move them to the place of his will. One such person is Rahab. She was described as a harlot, and her original situation was unacceptable to God. But as we read further, she proved herself diligent in providing protection to the spies that came to her house; she feared the God of Israel and his people (Joshua 2:1-22). Later in scripture, she appears in the lineage of Christ (Matthew 1:5), the place of God's will for her life. Abram was called to leave his homeland and travel to an unknown destination, Joseph was called to faithfully serve his masters while in Egypt long before he was eventually elevated to prime minister, and Moses was called to lead sheep before he would lead a multitude.

This section is an important reminder that as we journey to the place of God's will for our lives, we must work faithfully in the place where we stand at the present. Imagine someone saying, "I want to know God's will for my life," as they sit on a rock, calling upon God daily in prayer. My philosophy is to pray and keep moving, and when you get to where God wants you to be, he will let you know.

In a practical sense, this means for God's people to try new things, challenges, and adventures as he leads them along life's path. It means stepping out in spite of our fears and testing the waters to see if this thing or that is what he wants for us. How can one know that he is called to preach if he never tries? Remember the five indicators that were spoken of in section one: providence, passion, natural abilities, personality traits, and urging (calling). It is only in the process of moving and working in the place where we presently stand that these five indicators can reveal clues to help us to see God's will for our lives.

In my own life, I discovered my calling to ministry by going out on sick calls at hospitals, sitting in on Bible studies that were being taught, and studying along with the minister of the church where I attended. Had I not been willing to go out with him and do ministry, I would never have discovered God's will for my life to be a minister.

Man was not only created to work in his present situation, but, as stated earlier, he was made to bring glory to God. This purpose provides man with the understanding that not all endeavors or actions are God's will. No one can say, "Well, I am gifted at being a fast talker and being very cunning; therefore, it is God's will that I swindle people out of their money and possessions." Let it be understood that whatever we do, it must bring glory to God. Anything we undertake must never contradict that which is written in the Scripture that reveals God's will for how we ought to live. The Apostle Paul said it in a different manner, but the understanding is the same: "And whatsoever ye do in word or deed, do all in the name of the Lord Jesus, giving thanks to God and the Father by him" (Colossians 3:17, KJV).

This understanding should challenge every person who is seeking to know God's will for their lives to, in turn, test their own motives for why they want to do a certain thing. Let us consider some motives for why people do what they do: selfishness, greed, jealousy, envy, materialism, and pride. These are all bad reasons to want to pursue an endeavor, but it needs to be also understood that a person can pursue material things but have a pure motive that drives them. The prayer of Jabez demonstrates one who called upon God for a material increase, and God graciously granted the request:

> And Jabez called on the God of Israel, saying, Oh that thou wouldest bless me indeed, and enlarge my coast, and that thine hand might be with me, and that thou wouldest keep me from evil, that it may not grieve me! And God granted him that which he requested.
>
> 1 Chronicles 4:10 (KJV)

The love of money is evil, not money in itself. Every person who seeks a higher education does so in order to ensure themselves a better standard of living, which is not a wrong motive. But in that pursuit, we must never lose sight of a higher goal, and that is to please God and bring glory to him in the things we do. A powerful demonstration of this spirit is found in the life of Andrew Mizell Burton, who was wealthy yet used his wealth fully to the glory of God. In a biography of his life, it is stated:

> The business that he founded in 1903-the Life and Casualty Insurance Company of Tennessee-and over which he presided as president for forty-eight years is now one of the nation's largest and strongest insurance firms with nearly three billion dollars of insurance in force.
>
> A.M. Burton: http://www.therestoration-movement.com/burton,am.htm

He supported many Christian causes and the preaching of the gospel. Of particular note was his impact in the life of one of the country's greatest evangelists, Marshall Keeble. He freely funded brother Keeble's ministry, which allowed him the freedom to preach around the world the glorious gospel of Christ. A quote from the Biographical Sketch on the Life of Marshall Keeble says it best:

> Much can be said about the effect that Keeble had in his preaching and teaching. However he would have been the first to admit that much of his success was due to the empowerment he received both through the gospel and his life-long friendship with A. M. Burton. Burton, a fellow Christian, and owner of The Life and Casualty Company of Nashville, financed the work of Keeble from

> the early 1920s, and helped him in both his travels and his work for the rest of his life. The Bible and Burton gave Keeble the ability to make the world a better place.
>
> Keeble
>
> (http://www.therestorationmovement.com/keeble.htm)

This man used his wealth in a way that honored God. Wealth can be a wonderful tool in the hands of a faithful servant. Therefore, pursue whatever you desire so long as it is in keeping with God's written will for all of mankind, as given in Scripture.

Bringing glory to God means doing your best and always seeking to abide in his will. A great man, Martin Luther King Jr., once said:

> If a man is called to be a streetsweeper, he should sweep streets even as Michelangelo painted, or Beethoven composed music, or Shakespeare wrote poetry. He should sweep streets so well that all the hosts of heaven and earth will pause to say, here lived a great streetsweeper who did his job well.
>
> Martin Luther King Jr.
>
> (http://www.famousquotesandauthors.com/authors/martin_luther_king_jr_quotes.html)

The Apostle Paul exhorted the saints with the same:

> And whatsoever ye do, do it heartily, as to the Lord, and not unto men; knowing that of the Lord ye shall receive the reward of the inheritance: for ye serve the Lord Christ.
>
> Colossians 3:23–24 (KJV)

It is most helpful to me to remember two scriptures that guide me and keep me on the right path as I journey through life:

> Neither yield your members as instruments of unrighteousness unto sin: but yield yourselves unto God as those that are alive from the dead, and your members as instruments of righteousness unto God.
>
> Romans 6:13 (KJV)

> But in a great house there are not only vessels of gold and of silver, but also of wood and of earth; and some to honor, and some to dishonor. If a man therefore purge himself from these, he shall be a vessel unto honor, sanctified, and meet for the master's use, and prepared unto every good work.
>
> 2 Timothy 2:20-21 (KJV)

As God leads you to new avenues, situations, and vistas, keep these thoughts always before you: you are his instrument and vessel, and as his instrument and vessel, your goal is to bring him glory and accomplish his will.

The Resistance Factor

Ezekiel spoke of the potter and the clay; Paul spoke of the foolishness of the clay, defying the potter or arguing the choices of the potter. Both of these references point out the folly of resisting the hand of God as he moves in the lives of his people. Yet multitudes have found themselves fighting against God as he sought to fulfill his will for their lives. Even the most devout child of God may unwittingly find themselves resisting God by ignoring his movements or by failing to become still and rest in what may be uncomfortable and unpleasant times.

How then do we move unwittingly against God? We move this way by taking matters into our own hands, but we do it without an evil motive. It can be considered a friendly way of helping God along in fulfilling his will for our lives. Abraham and Sarah did this as they waited for the fulfillment of the promise of a child in their advanced years. There was no evil intent on either one's part, but they hatched and carried out a plot to help God along. As these servants grew impatient, this act was a move against the will of God and, in reality, a resisting of his will. The child that was born from this scheme would not be the promised seed of which God had spoken. In fact, he later told Abram directly that the child of this union, whose name was Ishmael, would not be his heir:

> Wherefore she said unto Abraham, Cast out this bond woman and her son: for the son of this bondwoman shall not be heir with my son, even with Isaac…and God said unto Abraham, Let it not be grievous in thy sight because of the lad, and because of thy bondwoman; in all that Sarah hath said unto thee, hearken unto her voice; for in Isaac shall thy seed be called.
>
> Genesis 21:11–12 (KJV)

In their haste and impatience, we see the mistake that these two icons of the Bible made. We want so badly for the thing that God has for us to come to pass and are too impatient to wait on his timing. We rush ahead of God in an effort to speed up his promises and will for our lives and, in the process, wreak havoc in our own lives and the lives of others.

There are two biblical characters that readily come to mind of people that resisted the will of God for their lives by both intentional actions and by refusing to rest and allow God to work in times that felt uncomfortable: King Saul and Jeroboam. One was intentional in his actions, and the other failed to rest and trust God in the face of uncomfortable and unpleasant times.

First, there was King Saul, who moved against God with full knowledge of his defiant actions. The scriptures tell us that God had a plan for Saul's life. He was called to serve as Israel's first king from a tribe not spoken of as being one from which Israel's kings would come. Jacob prophesied as he neared death that Israel's kings would be from the tribe of Judah: "The scepter shall not depart from Judah, nor a lawgiver from between his feet, until Shiloh come; and unto him shall the gathering of the people be" (Genesis 49:10, KJV). But here we have Saul, from the tribe of Benjamin. Remember at the beginning of the book, we discussed providence. Providence is when things happen to you that you did not orchestrate on your own. God moved providentially in Saul's life for him to become Israel's king and the anointed of God. We do not know God's full plans for Saul, but we do know he chose him to be king, and the only thing that short circuited the plan God had for him was his own willful disobedience.

A day came when God, through his prophet Samuel, gave specific instructions to his anointed servant, King Saul. One of Saul's purposes as king that God ordained for him was to save and deliver Israel from its enemies: "Anoint him to be captain over my people Israel that he may save my people out of the hand of the Philistines" (1 Samuel 9:16, KJV). He started well but finished poorly in following the will of God for his life. Saul did fight against and defeated the Philistines as instructed, but later he failed to obey God, and for this defiant act, he sidetracked what God had ordained for him. Samuel came to Saul and told him to fight against another enemy, the Amalekites:

> Now go and smite Amalek, and utterly destroy all that they have, and spare them not; but slay both man and woman, infant and suckling, ox and sheep, camel and ass.
>
> 1 Samuel 15:3 (KJV)

The text later says rather than completely annihilating the Amalekite enemy as instructed, he spared the king, the best sheep, other choice animals, and precious items. After Samuel discovered the defiant act, the words that he spoke declares how Saul resisted God's will by his disobedience: "And Samuel said unto Saul, I will not return with thee: for thou hast rejected the word of the lord, and the Lord hath rejected thee from being king over Israel" (1 Samuel 15:26, KJV).

It is a real possibility that we can resist God's will for our lives by willful disobedience. This does not mean that all is lost and that we are doomed to eternal damnation but that we may never experience the fullness of what he intends for us when we resist him with such intentional actions.

Another character, Jeroboam, failed to be still and rest in what was an uncomfortable and unpleasant time. Like he did with Saul, God again dispatched a prophet to declare his will for this man's life:

> And it came to pass at that time when Jeroboam went out of Jerusalem, that the prophet Ahijah the Shilonite found him in the way; and he had clad himself with a new garment; and they two were alone in the field: And Ahijah caught the new garment that was on him, and rent it in twelve pieces: And he said to Jeroboam, Take thee ten pieces: for thus saith the Lord, the God of Israel, Behold, I will rend the kingdom

> out of the hand of Solomon, and will give ten tribes to thee.
>
> 1 Kings 11:29–31 (KJV)

God's will for Jeroboam was for him to reign over ten tribes, and what an honor it must have been for him to be chosen for such a task. But as so many of God's people do, he made a dreadful mistake in not being patient enough to be still and wait on God in the midst of difficult and challenging times. If you read further into chapter 12, you will find that all of Israel was under the heavy burden of taxation imposed by Rehoboam, son of King Solomon. This burden made life difficult for the people to the extent that they were at the point of rebellion. The times were difficult indeed, but of all the people, Jeroboam should have been the one to remain at peace and stand still to wait for the salvation of the Lord. The establishment of Jeroboam's kingdom had been assured by the prophet Ahijah. His inability to stand still in challenging times led to him eventually resisting God's will for his life.

He moved on his own accord to make the prophecy a fulfillment by following the rebellion of the people and becoming their king. He went further against the will of God by establishing a false worship system: establishing two alternate places of worship, erecting false gods, and appointing an unapproved priestly system. How close he came to realizing God's will for his life; if only he could have been patient enough to wait, be still, and let God do the driving.

It is our tendency to want to run; it is the fight or flight response in us that makes it difficult to wait in troubling times. How many men and women wish they could go back and do things all over again? If only they had waited; they now see things would be so different and so much better.

Some practical things to remember in times like these are: First, obey God in all things; never become presumptuous in thinking you know what is best; check with him frequently in prayer. Second, when you are beginning to feel anxious, read the Word of God to see how he unfolded his will in the lives of biblical people. I like what Paul said, and it is appropriate at this time: "For whatsoever things were written aforetime were written for our learning, that we through patience and comfort of the scriptures might have hope" (Romans 15:4, KJV).

In times of doubt, run to him; in times of fear, cling to him; and in times of adversity, call upon him and he will be there, for he has said, "I will never leave thee, nor forsake thee" (Hebrews 13:5, KJV).

Nothing Just Happens

As cars go down the roadway and pass us, we have an opportunity to read many bumper stickers presenting various messages. One sticker said, "Life happens." Well, that's not really true; nothing just happens in the lives of people. I believe that the Bible declares that God moves in the lives of men and directs their paths.

One great example of the foolishness of thinking that God is not involved in human affairs stands boldly in the scriptures. An Old Testament account is given of a king who put too much stock in himself and none in God. God got his attention through a miraculous event and thereby forever changed his perspective on the workings of God in human history. The prophet Daniel recorded the bold and misguided words of King Nebuchadnezzar: "The king spake, and said, Is not this great Babylon, that I have built for the house of the kingdom by the might of my power, and for the honor of my majesty?" (Daniel 4:30, KJV)

How shortsighted it is for men to think all that is in his life is under his own control. How can he guide and control his own life when he doesn't even know what faces him the next moment? This king spoke out of ignorance and arrogance, but he learned a valuable lesson that forever changed him. As you reflect upon your own life, how often have you been tempted to think that you have the situation under control only to realize how out of control things really were?

The longing within us has been smoldering for a long time, even from our early years as toddlers when we wanted independence and as we grew older and wanted to do things ourselves. Do you remember that longing for independence? The lesson, as this book is read, is that we don't know the way, we don't know how to do it ourselves, and we need God to direct our paths.

I believe that as a loving Father who desires that we neither injure ourselves nor waste precious energy on unprofitable enterprises, God will bring events into our lives to wake us up to the reality that we need him. The sooner the lesson is learned, the better off we will be. King Nebuchadnezzar received his life-changing event when God spoke these words:

> While the word was in the king's mouth, there fell a voice from heaven, saying, O king Nebuchadnezzar, to thee it is spoken; the kingdom is departed from thee. And they shall drive thee from men, and thy dwelling shall be with the beast of the field: they shall make thee to eat grass as oxen, and seven times (literally seven years) shall pass over thee, until thou know that the most High ruleth in the kingdom of men, and giveth it to whomsoever he will.
>
> Daniel 4:31–32 (KJV)

What a scene it was to see this man lose his mind and become as an animal, live in the wild, and allow his appearance through neglect to be as a wild beast. For seven years, the king roamed the fields, thinking and acting as a lowly beast, until he became fully aware that he was not in control of anything—not even his own mind. After the stated period, God allowed his reasoning to return to him, and he saw things in a much different light:

> And at the end of the days I Nebuchadnezzar lifted up mine eyes unto heaven, and mine understanding returned unto me, and I blessed the most High, and I praised and honored him that liveth for ever, whose dominion is an everlasting dominion, and his kingdom is from generation to generation.
>
> Daniel 4:34 (KJV)

Nebuchadnezzar came to understand that nothing just happens; God is in control of all things, even when we are not aware of this great fact. The Apostle Paul, in his discourse with Athenians, echoed the sovereignty of God in the affairs of men with these words:

> And hath made of one blood all nations of men for to dwell on all the face of the earth, and hath determined the times before appointed, and the bounds of their habitation.
>
> Acts 17:26 (KJV)

God's sovereignty over our lives is complete. If we resist him, we suffer because of our folly, as did Pharaoh. If we submit to him, we are blessed and enjoy the full and abundant life that Christ spoke of: "The thief cometh not, but for to steal, and to kill, and to destroy: I am come that they might have life, and have it more abundantly" (John 10:10, KJV).

A spiritual battle is being waged between God and Satan for the hearts and souls of humanity, and, unfortunately, this reality escapes many. It is a struggle for dominance; one fights to give us life and freedom, the other to enslave us and ultimately to destroy us. Christ revealed this spiritual struggle to Peter and encouraged him with the knowledge that Christ himself would be in prayer for him. On one occasion he told him:

> And the Lord said, Simon, Simon, behold, Satan hath desired to have you, that he may sift you as wheat: But I have prayed for thee, that thy faith fail not: and when thou art converted, strengthen thy brethren.
>
> Luke 22:31–32 (KJV)

There is a stark difference between the two powers that are vying for us—God lovingly encourages and draws us, but Satan, on the other hand, lures, deceives, and entraps his prey. Hosea illustrated in moving words God's tender actions toward us as he seeks to lead us through life: "I drew them with cords of a man, with bands of love: and I was to them as they that take off the yoke on their jaws, and I laid meat unto them" (Hosea 11:4, KJV). As you read the words, I'm sure that a tender scene breaks across your mind, and you can envision him gently leading, freeing, and feeding those who would come.

The other scene is not so tender but one of fear, violence, and trickery. Peter stated: "Be sober, be vigilant; because your adversary the devil, as a roaring lion, walketh about, seeking whom he may devour" (1 Peter 5:8, KJV). This entity does not seek our benefit but our destruction, and, unfortunately, many willingly follow him. The truth is that we will follow one or the other, and this again stresses the truth that nothing just happens. God has not left us defenseless, but neither will he force us to follow him; he has given us a choice. The decision that we make determines who will be our master, God or Satan. Listen to the Apostle Paul:

> Know ye not, that to whom ye yield yourselves servants to obey, his servants ye are to whom ye obey; whether of sin unto death, or of obedience unto righteousness?
>
> Romans 6:16 (KJV)

The beauty in this is that every believer has made a decision to be free:

> But God be thanked, that ye were the servants of sin, but ye have obeyed from the heart that form of doctrine which was delivered you. Being then made free from sin, ye became the servants of righteousness.
>
> Romans 6:17–18 (KJV)

Although we made a choice to serve God and thus became his servants, our service is not a burden, for he has said:

> Come unto me all ye that labor and are heavy lade, and I will give you rest. Take my yoke upon you, and learn of me; for I am meek and lowly in heart: and ye shall find rest unto your souls. For my yoke is easy and my burden is light.
>
> Matthew 11:28–30 (KJV)

This service that we are enlisted in comes with a mission and work. God created us for his purposes of bringing glory to himself and fulfilling his will for the world. Someone said, "The only hands that God has are your hands." This is the importance of understanding God's will for your life so that you can fulfill your purpose for which you have been called.

Jeremiah's calling and purpose was determined before his birth, and so was ours: "Before I formed thee in the belly, I knew thee; and before thou camest forth out of the womb I sanctified thee, and I ordained thee a prophet unto the nations" (Jeremiah 1:5, KJV). But what troubles many is the fact that they may not know God's will for their lives. I believe that by following the steps revealed in this book, we can come closer than ever at knowing God's will for our lives. Unlike Jeremiah, we will not hear the audible voice of God to declare his will, but I am sure he has given us glimpses and indicators that will help us to have a greater assurance about where he wants us to be as we travel through life.

Finally, the question comes: "How do I yield to God and allow him to have control of my life?" I believe that three actions must occur in our hearts before he can lead us and truly reveal his will: humility of heart, a trusting heart, and a heart that is ready to surrender.

1. Humility of heart.

   God cannot work in a heart that is haughty and prideful. There is no room for him, and such a mind is not open to hear him. Have you ever dealt with a prideful, boastful person? Did you get anywhere? Case closed! Peter echoes the heart of God as it relates to a prideful verses a humble heart:

   > And be clothed with humility: for God resisteth the proud, and giveth grace to the humble. Humble yourselves therefore under the mighty hand of God, that he may exalt you in due time.
   >
   > 1 Peter 5:5–6 (KJV)

   Humility is vital to being led and taught. We can never know anything from God or man if we refuse to humble ourselves.

2. A trusting heart.

   Trust is the factor that will keep you moving in spite of adversity. Trust causes us to move when there is no apparent reason to do so. Abram believed (trusted) and moved out, heading to a foreign land yet unknown to him. Trust is a needed commodity as we seek the will of God because not everything will be as clear, and in those times, we must trust him. Job's words are ever true: "Though he slay me, yet will I trust in him…" (Job 13:15, KJV). Trust and obey are the words of the old song we all know so well, and it is appropriate for those who seek God's will for their lives.

3. A surrendered heart.

The thought that comes to my mind when I think of the word surrender is the scenes from old westerns. The house is surrounded by the sheriff and his posse, and the bad guys are told, "Come out with your hands up." Surrender is like that. It means giving up and letting God have his way in your life. Maybe you had plans for your life, but as God begins to knock at the door of your heart, you then realize that your plans and his are different; which way will you now go? Paul said that God has begun a work and will complete it: "Being confident of this very thing, that he which hath begun a good work in you will perform it until the day of Jesus Christ" (Philippians 1:6, KJV). This process cannot happen unless we surrender completely without reservations to the Lord.

As we seek to surrender, I would like to suggest three exercises we need to engage in regularly that will help us to give up and allow God to have his way. First, read the Word of God to discover his mind. Second, pray and ask for his guidance and the strength to follow in times of uncertainty and fear. Third, listen as you read the Word; he will speak to you. Listen to others that God may bring into your life; they may have a message from God that will bless you. They may reveal things they see in you that you may not see for yourself. Caution! Be careful that if they tell you something that is supposedly from the scriptures that it is, in fact, from the scriptures and has been rightly divided. Remember opinions are fine but not binding; don't let another person paint you into a corner. Keep your mind open to hear, but remember always, "Prove all things; hold fast to that which is good" (1 Thessalonians 5:2, KJV).

Conclusion

I have to ponder how many millions have gone through life before us and will follow who have wondered, "Lord, what is your will for my life?" These pages have been written with the purpose in mind to hopefully bring peace and an understanding to those who ask this question. If someone were to ask, "Can we know with certainty God's exact will?" the answer would be no, but Joseph would have had to answer in the same way. It was not until many years after being in Egypt and enduring many trials that he came to a realization of God's will. If we take the time to look at what God has revealed, how he has moved us along through life, the people he has brought our way, and the talents he has given us, I believe we can get a glimpse of his will and have a measure of peace in knowing we are where he wants us and are doing the things he desires for us.

My wish for you is that you may have that peace and consolation of knowing that you are where God wants you. May his peace be with you, may his Spirit guide you, and may you find yourself working in his vineyard until he comes again to receive his own unto himself.

Bibliography

C. F. Keil and F. Delitzsch, *Commentary on the Old Testament*, Peabody, Massachusetts, Hendrickson Publishers, Inc., 1996

Donna Partow, *Becoming a Vessel God Can Use,* Minneapolis, Minnesota: Bethany House, 1996

Edith Dean, *All of the Women of the Bible*, New York, New York: Harper & Row, 1955

George B. Caird, John C. Schroeder, *The Interpreter's Bible, the First and Second Books of Samuel*, Abingdon-Cokesbury Press, New York, Nashville, 1953

Hannah Hurnards, *Hinds' Feet on High Places,* Wheaton, Illinois: Tyndale House, 1975

Homer Hailey, *A Commentary on the Minor Prophets*, Amos, "Burden Bearer," Baker Book House, Grand Rapids, Michigan, 1972

John J. Davis, *Moses and the Gods of Egypt*, Grand Rapids, Michigan, Baker Book House, 1971

John J. Davis, John C. Whitcomb, *A History of Israel, from Conquest to Exile*, Grand Rapids, Michigan, Baker Book House, 1980

Reader's Digest, *Great People of the Bible and How They Lived*, The Reader's Digest Association, Inc. Pleasantville, New York, 1974

Robert Alter, *The David Story, A Translation with Commentary of 1 and 2 Samuel*, W. W. Norton & Company Inc., New York, New York, 1999

Robert Jamieson, A. R. Fausset and David Brown, Published 1871

Internet Resources

A.M. Burton: http://www.therestorationmovement.com/burton,am.htm

Adam Clarke, Clarke's Commentary http://www.studylight.org/com/acc/

http://www.Biblestudytools.com/commentaries/jamieson-fausset-brown/

Keeble: http://www.therestorationmovement.com/keeble.htm

Martin Luther King Jr.: http://www.famousquotesandauthors.com/authors/martin_luther_king_jr_quotes.html